YOUTH WORK

READY-TO-USE MEETING GUIDE

OMNIBUS EDITION

YOUTH WORK

READY-TO-USE MEETING GUIDE

OMNIBUS EDITION

John Buckeridge

Designed by Rachel Salter

KINGSWAY PUBLICATIONS

EASTBOURNE

First published in four separate volumes in 1994 and 1995.
This Omnibus Edition first published 1996.

ISBN 0 85476 710 X

Photos: Chris Gander, Luke Golobitsh, Jim Loring
Illustrations: Ian Long
Text design: Rachel Salter

Book 1. 'Every Second Counts' devised by Peter Meadows for use in the main seminars at Spring Harvest 1994 and used with his permission.

Book 2: The meeting outline for Chapter 7 was written by John Allan and is used with his permission.

Book 3: A significant part of the 'Selling Power' meeting plan was written by Kevin Elliott and is used with his permission. The 'New Age' meeting plan was written by John Allan and is used with his permission. 'Alcohol - the Facts' from the 'Booze Up' meeting plan was adapted from material supplied by the UK Band of Hope and is used with their permission. The quote on the drug Ecstasy by Jay from the 'Drugs' meeting plan is from an article called 'User Friendly' written by Alex Spillius which appeared in the 'Life' supplement of *The Observer*, 23 October 1994.

Book 4: This material was co-written by John Allan and John Buckeridge. The text of the Apostles' Creed (adapted) is copyright 1970, 1971, 1975, the International Consultation on English Texts (ICET).

Scripture quotations are from the *Good News Bible* © American Bible Society 1976, published by the Bible Society and HarperCollins; the *New International Version* 1973, 1978, 1984 by the International Bible Society; and *The Message*, a paraphrase of the Scriptures by Eugene H. Peterson © 1993, Navpress USA.

Designed and produced by Bookprint Creative Services, P.O. Box 827, BN21 3YJ, England, for KINGSWAY PUBLICATIONS LTD
Lottbridge Drove, Eastbourne, East Sussex BN23 6NT.
Printed in Great Britain.

CONTENTS

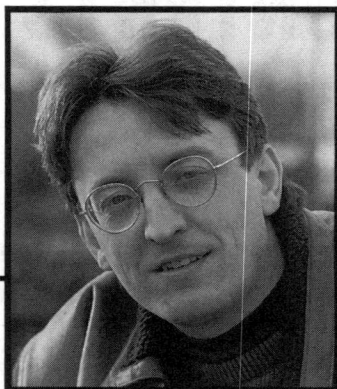

How to Use This Book

This material has been designed to be used with 12 to 16-year-olds. That doesn't mean it can't work with younger or older youngsters, but then it will probably need to be adapted and changed.

No two groups of young people are the same, therefore although these meeting plans are designed to be 'ready to use', you will need to adapt some of the material to make it work really well with your own particular group of young people.

The sessions can be used in four series, but will work just as well as individual units. In fact you may find that some of the units contain too much for just one week. The key thing is to adapt and personalise the material to take into account your own gifting, available resources and the needs of your young people.

Most of the units include icebreaker games, discussion starters and other interaction elements. It is important to avoid too much 'chalk and talk' style teaching. Young people learn best through a mix of learning elements.

The reproducible sheets vary in form and content. They use a mix of styles to stimulate Bible study, discussion and reflection on the meeting theme. You are free to photocopy these for local church use. This does not apply to large-scale events where over 100 people are expected.

As well as the reproducible sheets there are also publicity pages with illustrations for you to use to publicise the first meeting in each term-long series.

Please do prepare well. Although this book is designed to take some of the hard work and hassle out of preparation, you will still need to read through the meeting plan at least a couple of days beforehand. This will give you time to collect any props or other equipment you need as well as Bibles, pens and copies of the repro-sheet.

This book was written in response to requests to me at YOUTH**WORK** magazine from youth leaders/workers. The call was for more of the Ready-To-Use Meeting pages from the magazine – well, here they are! I'd be interested to get your feedback, both positive and negative, so any further books can take your comments into consideration. Write to me at YOUTH**WORK** Magazine, 37 Elm Road, New Malden, Surrey KT3 3HB. If you haven't seen a copy of YOUTH**WORK** or would like to subscribe, check out the advertisement on pages 102-3.

John Buckeridge

Book One: Christian Basics

It is sometimes easy to assume that the young people in your group are all familiar with the basics of Christianity, and that to go over old ground will only bore them. But we all benefit from a fresh look at the foundations of our faith. What do we believe about God? Do we have the right idea about the Bible? Do we understand what sin is? And forgiveness...?

Here are some fast-moving sessions suitable for young people who are new to the church, and those who think they have 'heard it all before'.

Be careful to do your preparation well. Don't assume that because you are dealing with basics you already know all there is to know. Ask God for some new insights and be prepared to answer some hard questions.

READY-TO-USE-MEETING GUIDE

Get your meeting noticed by using the ready-to-photocopy artwork below to promote the first week of this term-long series of meetings. Simply add the details of venue and time and photocopy onto paper or thin coloured card. This image can be shrunk in size to use as a personal invite or expanded to poster size to pin onto a notice board at church, school, youth club etc.

BRING AN EMPTY STOMACH AND A QUESTIONING MIND

Check it Out

FEED YOUR GUT and FEED YOUR MIND

Join us ↓

INVESTIGATE THE CLAIMS OF CHRISTIANITY 4 YOURSELF

CHECK IT OUT

MEETING AIM:
To encourage young people to begin to investigate the Christian faith.

TASTE AND SEE (10 mins)
Buy at least eight packets of different flavoured crisps. Before the young people arrive empty each packet into a bowl and number the bowls one to eight. Keep a careful record of which flavour is in which bowl.

As the young people arrive give them each a pen and small sheet which lists the eight flavours. They must correctly match up each flavour with the correct number. Make sure you buy some similar flavours such as Beef, Marmite, and Beef and Onion to add to the confusion - plus of course the old favourites like Salt and Vinegar and Cheese and Onion.

SUPER SARNIES (10-15 mins)
Some strange combinations of foods work well together. A banana and jam sandwich may sound disgusting, but it tastes great! This game provides a chance to experiment with 15 different food flavours.

Give everyone the chance to make two experimental sandwiches with a maximum of three filling mixtures in each.

Suggested fillings are; strawberry jam, marmite, cheddar cheese slices, cream cheese, honey, brown sugar, chocolate spread, slices of banana, tuna, sliced tomato, peanut butter, raisins, mustard, cold sliced sausage, shredded lettuce, walnuts, cress, luncheon meat slices, onion rings, sweetcorn, finely sliced celery. Don't forget you will also need sufficient bread and margarine.

Encourage individuals to come up with creative names for their new sarnie combos.

Appoint a taste test committee of three young people and a leader/helper to decide on the tastiest combination and the weirdest taste mixture.

If you feel like being generous, give a McDonalds meal voucher to the maker of the best sarnie.

TASTE AND SEE (5 mins)
Read Psalm 34:8-10 in a modern translation.
SAY: 'I believe it is important that people think through for themselves and test out what the Christian faith is all about.
'Just as you needed to taste each crisp before you could decide on its flavour - and how seemingly weird combinations of sandwich filling sometimes tasted good when you checked them out - in the same way, it's easier to come to a conclusion about whether Christianity is true or not by checking it out for yourself. Many people dismiss it without investigating the facts, reading the Bible, praying to God etc.

MY LIFE SO FAR... (15 mins)
Hand out copies of the sheet opposite and a pen/pencil. Ask everyone to fill in the boxes with the significant things that happened to them at that age/stage of development. Allow about five minutes for this.

Allow time for everyone to feedback what they wrote. Use this as a way to get to know your group better.

WALKING ON WATER (15 mins)
Turn down the lights and/or draw the curtains so the room is darkish, but light enough for you to read.

Explain that you are going to read out a story from the Bible and appoint everyone a character from the story. For every six people in the group appoint one to be Jesus, one to be Peter and the rest assorted disciples.

Then carefully explain the context of the reading and take time to encourage each person to 'get into their character from the story'.

Read Matthew 14:22-34 slowly - pausing between verses to allow the impact of the story to have an effect. You may want to read it through a second time. Then ask the group to describe how they felt and thought during the story, in particular get them to verbalise:
- How the disciples felt when Jesus first appeared.
- How Peter felt when he stepped out of the boat.
- The disciple's reaction to Peter's decision to get out of the boat and what the other disciples expected to happen next.
- Peter's reaction when he started walking on water.
- Jesus' reaction to Peter's decision to get out of the boat.
- Why Peter started to sink.
- What Jesus was thinking when Peter was sinking.
- The thoughts/reactions of all the characters in the story once everyone was back on dry land.
- Do the disciples think of Jesus in a different way following this miracle? If so, how?

MODERN-DAY MIRACLES (10 mins)
Ask if any of them have ever had a prayer answered, seen a miracle, asked God for healing, etc. Encourage open discussion and sharing.

Most people have prayed to God at a moment of crisis or difficulty. John McCarthy, a British journalist kidnapped in Lebanon in the 1980s, asked for help from God during a particularly bleak moment during his long captivity. He did not consider himself a Christian, or religious, but in the book *Some Other Rainbow* he records 'The next instant I was standing up, surrounded by a warm bright light. I was dancing full of joy. In the space of a minute, despair had vanished, replaced by boundless optimism.'

Most times when people pray a 'God help me' type prayer, even if God answers they tend to forget about him.

Emphasise that God is interested in developing a relationship with us, rather than only being contacted when we are in an emergency.

BEEN THERE, DONE IT (10 mins)
Invite a Christian to come and briefly share their testimony about how they came to faith in Jesus (alternatively it could be one of the young people or you). Encourage the person to be totally honest, and open it up for questions from the young people.
The testimony does not necessarily have to be a highly dramatic, 'I used to be a drug-taking, sex-mad, rock 'n' roll star' account, to make a big impression.

Conclude by saying that hearing about someone's personal experience of God isn't conclusive evidence but it is important and it should be carefully considered.

OPTIONAL EXTRA
Pray and look for opportunities during this evening or at a later date to ask individuals who are not Christians what it would take for them to believe in God and become a Christian and/or alternatively what is stopping them!

This needs to be delicately and diplomatically put, but could result in a significant conversation about their struggles, doubts or problems about the Christian faith.

WHAT IS GOD LIKE?

MEETING AIM:

To identify young people's perceptions of the nature of God and present the biblical view of him as a real, living, supreme person.

SPOT THE CELEB (10 mins)

Tear out photographs of celebrities from magazines and on a photocopier enlarge or shrink them to A4 size, then transfer the image onto an OHP acetate. You will need to use special acetates designed for this purpose - ordinary ones will melt in the photocopier!

Split the group into two equal teams and then announce that you will slowly reveal a picture of someone well known. They need to correctly identify the celebrity.

Put the first acetate with a backing mask onto the screen, then gradually draw back the masking paper to reveal more and more of the face.

As soon as someone from one of the teams shouts 'stop', you stop revealing more of the face and the team has 10 seconds to identify the person correctly (accept only the first answer). If they are wrong, the other team can see the whole face for their guess. Only if they guess wrong does the first team have another chance to identify the celeb.

This means that if a team shouts 'stop' before they are sure, they run the risk of handing the answer to the other team on a plate.

Use this and the following game to focus on the theme of identification.

KNOBBLY KNEE CONTEST (10 mins)

Ask for six volunteers - four lads, two girls. The girls are taken out of the room while the lads sit on a row of chairs and roll up their right trouser leg to above the knee.

The girls are blindfolded and led in one at a time. A helper guides them down the line of lads while they touch each knee in turn. The girls then attempt to identify which knee belongs to whom.

SYMBOLS QUIZ (10 mins)

Hand out pens and copies of the sheet opposite, and ask the group to work (as individuals or in small teams - you choose) through the symbols identifying what they each represent. Emphasise that they should not begin to complete the second half of the sheet (God Is...) even if they finish the quiz early.

ANSWERS: 1) Do not Bleach **2)** British Telecom **3)** HMV **4)** Water **5)** Mercedes-Benz **6)** Head **7)** Warm Iron **8)** Dispose of Litter in Bin **9)** Treble Clef **10)** Midland Bank **11)** UniChem **12)** The Body Shop **13)** Mercury Communications **14)** Apple Computer **15)** Birds Eye **16)** Abbey National **17)** Warner Brothers **18)** Wella **19)** Michelin **20)** Recyclable **21)** Yellow Pages **22)** Pure New Wool **23)** Renault **24)** Norwich Union **25)** Lacoste

ASK (3 mins)

Why are symbols so widely used?

(They represent a larger piece of information - they symbolise something, eg white flag = surrender.)

GOD IS... (15 mins)

Ask the group to draw a symbol on the bottom half of the photocopied sheet to represent their understanding/belief/unbelief of God. They are not allowed to use any words, lettering or numbers. The picture/graphic they draw should accurately represent what they think of God, eg a cloud to represent something hidden or mysterious. Emphasise that you are not looking for a work of art! Allow three minutes.

Ask the young people to show the rest of the group their symbol picture - group to feedback what they think the symbol means, *then* the 'artist' to say whether anyone correctly interpreted their symbolic drawing, and if not to explain it themselves.

SUPER SPY? (10 mins max.)

Give a short talk which identifies the main ideas that people have about God.

Super Spy - A nosy parker who has his eye on everyone so that he can punish you if you do something wrong.

Santa Claus - A kindly old man who gives you things if you are vaguely good. A bit out of touch, but someone to be honoured on special occasions like Christmas.

A Blob - Not a person but a 'force', a bit like lightning. Not someone you could form a relationship with or get to know personally.

The Doctor - Someone to call on in an emergency, but ignore when everything is going OK.

The Bible teaches that God is a real, living person who is a spirit. In small groups examine what else the Bible says God is like.

GOD STUDY (15 mins)

1) **ASK:** From what sources do we get our ideas of what God is like?

2) **READ:** John 14:5-10. What two things do we learn about what God is like from these verses? (God is a father figure, God made himself known to us as a man called Jesus).

3) **LIST:** as many qualities/characteristics of God that you can which are mentioned in the Bible, back this up with Bible verses wherever you can. If a group is struggling, point them to Psalm 8 and Psalm 24 for ideas.

IN MY EXPERIENCE (5 mins)

Prearrange with one of your young people, someone from church, one of your co-leaders (or you!) to give a short, three-minute testimony of their relationship with God and how they relate to him as a father/supreme being.

Give the young people the opportunity to ask questions.

WHERE ARE YOU? (10 mins)

Conclude by asking the young people to walk around the room and find a road sign which symbolises where they are at in their relationship with God. You will need to prepare a range of road signs beforehand (drawn or enlarged on a photocopier from a copy of the Highway Code).

Each person brings back a sign and explains in what way the sign symbolises their experience of God, eg the 'No Entry' sign could mean they feel cut off from God, the 'bumpy road' sign could signify they are going through a rough patch, or the '70mph' sign could represent that they feel they are making fast progress in their Christian life.

OPTIONAL EXTRA

Ask the group to write down the one question they would most like God to answer. Ask different group members to take it in turn to 'play God' and try to answer the question. Emphasise that it isn't wrong to ask God hard questions, and that even if we don't get an answer now, one day if we go to heaven, we will get the opportunity to ask God face to face.

H_2O

1........................ 2........................ 3........................ 4........................ 5........................

6........................ 7........................ 8........................ 9........................ 10........................

11........................ 12........................ 13........................ 14........................ 15........................

16........................ 17........................ 18........................ 19........................ 20........................

21........................ 22........................ 23........................ 24........................ 25........................

God is....

S I N

MEETING AIM

To help the group gain a clearer idea of the Bible's teaching about sin, the way it operates in human life, and God's solution to the problem. Main points: that sin is a nature, not just a series of wrong actions; that sin can be corporate as well as individual; that sin distorts the image of God in human life; that the Christian still possesses a sinful old nature; and that Christ came to destroy the power of sin by sacrificing himself.

HOLD THE FRONT PAGE (10 mins)

Divide the group into teams of four or five. Give each a pile of old newspapers, a pair of scissors, some glue and a photocopy of the Daily Blast worksheet opposite (you may want to enlarge it to A3 format).

They have five minutes to make their own newspaper front page by taking clippings from the old papers. They can include what they like, but they will be awarded different marks according to the stories they choose (eg 10 for a story of human depravity, 20 for a story of human goodness, 5 for a pessimistic forecast, 10 for an optimistic forecast, 5 for a crime/war story, 10 for a love story...).

This exercise should show how much more difficult it is to find hopeful, optimistic stories of goodness. Crime and evil are all over the place in many different forms. Why is this? Because of what the Bible calls sin.

THE GRAVITY TRAIN (5 mins)

Ask people to shout out the first word that crosses their mind when the word 'sin' is mentioned. Usually they will come up with a list of actions: thieving, adultery, murder etc. Make the point that these are just some of the *results* of sin - the fruit on the tree. The root of it is an evil bias fixed deep in the human nature.

Stand one volunteer on a chair, grasping one end of a broomstick. Another volunteer stands on the ground, behind a line drawn two feet in front of the chair, grasping the other end of the broomstick. Tell them that on no account are they to let go of the stick, but by twisting and pulling, the first volunteer is to try and pull the second over the line. The second has to try and pull the first off the chair.

Most times the person on the chair will lose. Gravity is a powerful force pulling us downwards and that's how the Bible says sin operates in our lives.

BIBLE CHECK (10 mins)

Read Romans 7:15-20, then get them to discuss the following questions in small groups:

● What are the two bizarre results that sin produces (v15)?
● What is it inside people that produces these results (v17-18)?
● What would Paul have said to people who claimed, 'I try my best - nobody can do more'?

Paul goes on to talk about sin in us as a 'law' just like gravity, pulling us down (v23). That doesn't mean we're not responsible for giving in to it! But it can sometimes be hard to work out who is to blame...

WHODUNNIT? (5 mins)

Write on an OHP acetate:

> **THOUSANDS HAVE DIED IN FORMER YUGOSLAVIA**
>
> **MY TEA WAS BURNT YESTERDAY EVENING**
>
> **THERE IS A FAMINE IN SUDAN**
>
> **I TOLD A LIE**
>
> **HENRY WAS ABUSED AS A CHILD AND NOW ABUSES CHILDREN HIMSELF**

ASK: who is responsible for each of these evil things? Some are simple to work out - others are more difficult.

Allow people to argue for a while, then say; sometimes you can't just find one individual to blame - sometimes blame has to be shared. Sometimes the evil is in the very structures of society, like when a repressive government denies basic human rights, or when a multinational corporation oppresses poor people to make massive profits for its shareholders.

That's the trouble with sin it spreads everywhere. Theologians speak about 'total depravity' - which means that every human

activity is twisted and tainted by sin.

TWISTED PICTURE (5 mins)

Show the group a slide picture (of anything you like). When it's projected, you see on the wall a perfect representation of what's on the film. In the same way, when we were created, we were a perfect representation of God's character - we were made in his image.

Now twist the lens. The picture becomes blurred and finally unrecognisable. Explain, that's what sin does, blur the image of God in people.

When someone becomes a Christian, the image of God is renewed. A new nature arrives which we never had before. But does that mean our struggles are over?

BACK TO THE BIBLE (10 mins)

In small groups, read Romans 8:5-11 and look for answers to these questions:

● What are the two forces fighting for control of a Christian's mind?
● We can give in to each of them. What is the difference in the results we'll get?
● If you are really a Christian, which force is invincible - and why?
● What's the answer to people who say, 'Christians are all hypocrites, pretending to be holier than thou'?

SIN BONFIRE (10 mins)

Give everyone paper and a pen. Ask them to think back over the past week and mark a tick on the paper for each time they can remember doing something sinful. Stress that they won't have to show this to anyone else! Then fold up all the papers and collect them in a heap on a Pyrex dish, and read out Hebrews 9:26b-28. Explain that we are sinners and will always be until we reach heaven, but that Easter won our freedom (1 Peter 3:18). God will not condemn us for our sins, or leave us powerless to overcome temptation.

Then, slowly and wordlessly, squirt lighter fuel over the pile of paper and set it alight. As it burns, pray together, thanking Jesus for dying on the cross and the liberation from sin's slavery that it brings.

THE DAILY BLAST

WHO IS JESUS?

MEETING AIM:

To introduce Jesus as a historical person who was both fully human and fully divine, and someone who is very different from the popular but largely mythical Christmas card/stained-glass image.

IDENTIKIT (10 mins)

Use this as an opening game or even as an intro game (as people arrive at the venue for the meeting). You will need to collect at least 25 photographs of very well-known pop-stars, sportsmen/women, TV/film personalities/actors, etc. Because their faces are so well known make it a bit harder to identify the person by cutting out just a small part of their face (eg eyes and nose) and then display these around the walls of the venue/room. Beside each part of face put a number. With a pad and pencil, the young people need to identify the stars from the photofit section of face shown.

Give a suitably crazy prize for the winner(s) eg, painting by numbers set, eye make-up kit, rubber face mask, eye patch, whodunnit detective novel.

MEEK AND MILD? (10 mins)

Collect a selection of pictures and illustrations depicting Jesus. These could include Christmas cards, postcards of oil paintings, religious pictures and statutes. Ask the young people to comment on the pictures and give an opinion of the sort of person these images portray.

Sum up by making the point that Jesus is considered by many to have been a wimpy, white-faced, blue-eyed man who wore a white sheet and ended up a victim. Make the point that the Bible does not portray him like that at all!

SPOT THAT MAN (15 mins)

Provide photocopies of the worksheet opposite, give 10 minutes for the activity and five minutes for feedback. You could also pin some/all of the completed worksheets onto the wall.

JESUS FAX QUIZ (5 mins)

Ask the group to divide up into teams of three. Then read out the following statements about Jesus. Allow 10 seconds' discussion in their threes then they need to decide if the statement is true or false. Ask them to keep a score and at the end ask them if they got more right than wrong.

1) Jesus has several half-brothers and sisters *(T)*.

2) Mary was no more than 19 when she gave birth to Jesus *(T)* [Not proven, but highly likely to be].

3) Instead of a cot the baby Jesus slept in an animal feeding trough *(T)*.

4) During his lifetime on earth Jesus travelled in a part of the Middle East no bigger than Wales *(T)*.

5) Jesus once told a story about 10 virgins *(T)*.

6) Jesus predicted the rise and fall of communism *(F)*.

7) There is more proof that Julius Caesar existed than Jesus *(F)*.

8) During his lifetime Jesus spent five times as many years working with wood as with people *(T)*.

9) At the time of his death Jesus had about 3,000 followers *(F)* [around 100].

10) Every day around 70,000 more people decide to become followers of Jesus *(T)*.

WHAT WOULD YOU DO? (10 mins)

Ask your group what they would do in the following situations, then get them to check out the Bible verses.

1) You are sitting on a park bench talking with your mates, when a group of little kids sit down and start listening in and then joining in on your conversation. Your friends tell the little kids to get lost. What do you do?
Now read Mark 10:13-16.

2) A group of lads about your age or older start picking on a girl three years younger than them. She is on her own. The lads ask you to join the bullying or risk getting picked on yourself. What do you do?
Now read John 8:1-11.

3) One of your best friends is spotted by a gang of people who don't like you. Your friend tells them he is not your friend, in fact he hardly even knows you. He shouts and swears to make his point. Then you get badly beaten up by this gang. The next time you see your (supposed) friend he wants to hang around with you and be your best mate. What do you do?
Now read Matthew 26:31-35; Mark 14:66-72; John 21:15-19.

FULLY HUMAN - FULLY GOD (10 mins)

SAY: 'Christians believe that Jesus was the Son of God and that he was at the same time fully human (cut him and he bleeds) AND fully God (perfect and holy).'

Divide your young people into two, hand out Bibles in a modern translation (preferably the same one) and get one group to read out loud the passages which highlight Jesus' humanness, and the second group to read out the passages which reveal that Jesus was the Son of God. After each reading, ask the group what human or divine qualities the reading demonstrates.

HUMAN	DIVINE
Matthew 26:36-38	John 10:30-33
John 4:5-8	Mark 7:27-30
John 11:28-36	John 11:38-48
Matthew 27:45-46	Matthew 27:50-54

YOUR STORY (5 mins)

Finish the session by telling the young people what Jesus means to you. Talk about how you became a Christian, what convinced you to follow Jesus and give examples of what following Christ has meant (both in terms of cost and benefits) in your life.

OPTIONAL EXTRAS

1) Show part of the *Jesus* video (available from Scripture Press/International Films for £19.95). This 120-minute film follows the life of Jesus. Alternatively you could hire or buy the much acclaimed *Jesus of Nazareth* which starred Robert Powell as Jesus and was directed by Franco Zeferrelli (available from most video stockists).

2) Get your group to make a banner which portrays one of the characteristics of Jesus. Alternatively, get them to draw/paint a Bayeux tapestry-style collage on a roll(s) of paper/wallpaper/backing paper for wallpaper. Display their work in the group/club room, at church, and at the next March For Jesus nearest you (you may need to carve up the long tapestry for this last idea!).

The religious leaders mostly hated Jesus and towards the end of this three-year preaching tour they wanted to kill him. Imagine that you are compiling a wanted poster for Jesus. From the gospel accounts and using a bit of discretion build up a profile of the man Jesus, eg skin colour, age, habits, regular places he visits, people he mixes with, aliases or other names, family background, occupation, likes and dislikes, personality/behaviour characteristics, plus any other relevant data.

WANTED

DEAD OR ALIVE

Jesus of Nazareth

If you see this man report his whereabouts at once to the Roman army or religious secret police force. On no account should you approach this man - he is highly dangerous and powerful.

....
....
....
....
....
....
....
....
....

REWARD:

For information leading to arrest and successful conviction the religious authorities will pay

30 pieces of silver!

HOLY SPIRIT

MEETING AIM:

To teach on aspects of the person and work of the Holy Spirit and to emphasise the importance of both the gifts and the fruit of the Holy Spirit. Also to encourage people to ask God to fill them, grow in the fruit and receive and exercise gifts of the Holy Spirit.

N.B. There is a lot of material in this session and you may want to divide it into two weeks.

BALLOON BREATH (10 mins)

Give everyone a balloon and ask them to blow it up so big that it bursts! After the pops of bursting balloons and laughter die down introduce the session with 'This week we are going to be looking at God's Holy Spirit. In the Old Testament the word used for "spirit" is "ruach" which literally means "breath" or "wind". When you breathed into your balloons they had life and energy. In the same way when the "ruach" or the Spirit of God fills us we have God's life and energy to live fulfilled and godly lives.

'The Bible also teaches that the Holy Spirit is not a force, but a person. He is part of God (Father, Son, Holy Spirit) and we are told not to grieve him and make him sad by stopping him work in our lives or by doing evil (Ephesians 4:30).'

NAME THAT FRUIT (10 mins)

Peel and cut into cubes a selection of fruits. You will need one cube of each fruit for everyone present. Have everyone sitting down in a pitch black room or have them blindfold.

Then feed a cube of the first fruit (eg, melon) to everyone. The lights go up for 10 seconds to allow them to write down what they thought the fruit was. Then turn off the lights and bring in the next fruit.

Use between six and 10 fruits in total, and be sure to include one or two unusual/exotic fruits as well as apple, banana, satsuma etc.

FRUIT OF THE SPIRIT (7 mins)

SAY: 'God's Holy Spirit is involved in our lives. He helps us to come to faith in Jesus, and when we become a Christian he lives inside us. He gives us the power to be Jesus' followers and St Paul writes that he encourages us to grow like fruit. Fruit takes time to mature into ripeness. In the same way as God's Spirit works in us, we will gradually become more and more mature - like Jesus. Paul lists what this fruit is in Galatians 5:22-26. We all need these qualities in our lives.'

ASK: the group to complete section one of the worksheet.

FILLED WITH THE SPIRIT (3 mins)

SAY: 'Although the Holy Spirit lives in us when we become Christians, God wants us to receive him in fullness and power.'

READ: Acts 8:14-17 as an example of people who believed in Jesus but had not been filled with the Holy Spirit. Make the point that this is an ongoing process. God wants us to go on asking him to fill us with his Spirit (Ephesians 5:18).

GET THE BALANCE (10 mins)

The props you need for this game are: two or more kitchen balance scales and a large number of parcels of differing weights.

Ideally you need a pair of scales for every four people. Prepare a large number of parcels (at least 20) which should all be a slightly different weight from each other, up to 3lbs in weight.

By putting different things in different parcels - eg paper, a brick, a balloon, they will differ in shape as well as weight. Finally make up two parcels which are identical in weight. Then number each parcel clearly with a different number.

The game requires each group to attempt to discover the two parcels which are identical in weight. They do this by selecting two parcels from the pile and weighing them on the scale to see if they balance. If they think they have the perfect match they shout out the two numbers to you, to discover if they are right. At the end of the game say: 'Some Christians emphasise the importance of the fruit of the Spirit, while others emphasise the gifts of the Spirit. The truth is that both are of equal importance and need to be kept in balance. We need to be demonstrating the fruit of the Spirit (love, joy, peace, patience etc) and we need to be exercising the gifts of the Spirit (prophecy, tongues, faith etc).

FLOUR FEAR (15 mins)

Fill a small round pudding bowl with flour. Use a knife to level off the flour in the bowl, pressing it down well. Then put a large flat plate or stiff piece of card onto the bowl. Turn the bowl over and carefully lift the bowl up so that the flour stays in a moulded shape. Then carefully put a chocolate finger biscuit into the top of the flour pie.

The group take it in turn to shave a piece off the edge of the flour with a blunt knife without causing the finger biscuit to slip/fall off. The daring slice a large segment away.

This continues with the fear factor of failure mounting as the flour pie gets smaller and smaller, until someone disturbs the biscuit. They must then pick out the biscuit from the crumbled pie with their teeth. This isn't easy, especially if someone helpfully pushes their head into the flour at the wrong moment!

Talk about the game and how the tension and apprehension grew. Then explain that a lot of Christians are apprehensive or even fearful of the Holy Spirit, and in particular the 'Gifts of the Spirit'. Ask the group what sort of things people are afraid of concerning the Holy Spirit, and in particular, the gifts.

GIFTS OF THE SPIRIT (7 mins)

SAY: 'Although the Holy Spirit is himself a gift, he wants to give us more. The gifts of the Spirit are for every Christian and Paul says we should eagerly want them (1 Corinthians 14:1). The different gifts are listed in 1 Corinthians 12:1-11 and are designed to build us up in our faith and to build up the church.

'Sometimes people are afraid of these gifts. They are afraid that maybe they will lose control when the Holy Spirit fills them or gives them a gift. This is not the case. The Holy Spirit is gentle and will not force us to do anything we don't want to do.

ASK: the group to complete section three of the worksheet.

QUESTIONS, QUESTIONS (10-20 mins)

You may want to give a whole extra week to explaining the use and function of the gifts of the Spirit described in 1 Corinthians 12:4-11. If not, briefly make the following points and allow time for questions about what you have covered so far.

☛ **Wisdom** - not logic, but supernatural wisdom - an insight into a problem that seemed to have no answer.

☛ **Word of knowledge** - God revealing something about a person/situation.

☛ **Faith** - confidence in God's ability to

heal/speak/do something out of the ordinary.

☛ **Healing** - supernatural healing in body, emotions or mind.

☛ **Miracles** - dramatic signs and deeds.

☛ **Prophecy** - spoken to strengthen, encourage and comfort. Sometimes predicts a future event. Can take various forms, eg, vision, spoken word, drama. Must always be carefully tested and considered. Should always be in line with existing revelation (Bible).

☛ **Discerning Spirits** - noticing the presence of evil spirits.

☛ **Tongues** - ability to speak to God in a language you haven't learned. Can be used in praise and/or intercession. Two areas of use: i) Private - helps you grow spiritually (1 Corinthians 4:2), ii) Public - spoken out loud which then requires interpretation.

☛ **Interpretation of tongues** - able to explain a message in tongues given in public. Not a translation, but gives the basic message/heart of what is said. A tongue in private to God does not need interpretation.

NB - The gifts often work together, eg Ananias (Acts 9:1-18) who used prophecy, visions, healing and faith together.
– We need to use and practise the gifts to become more fluent.

BEING FILLED

These things can be a block and prevent God from filling us with the Holy Spirit. Therefore they need to be confessed/dealt with:● Not a Christian. ● Unconfessed sin. ● Feelings of fear, hurt or rejection. ● Previous involvement with occult, eg ouija, tarot, levitation.

Allow a moment of silence for people to get right with God, confess sin etc.

In an atmosphere of worship pray – ask the Holy Spirit to come and fill, empower, encourage fruit and give gifts. Get the group to pray for each other in small groups with a leader present in each group. Encourage them to share if a particular gift is wanted, then pray together. Afterwards in your small groups share what prayers were said/requests made. Keep the atmosphere of worship alive, you may want to continue to sing songs, play a worship tape etc.

Be sensitive to what is going on and only then decide how best to close the session. Be sure to follow up on this session through one-to-one contact. Encourage the young people who received a gift (tongues, prophecy etc) and give them opportunities to exercise this gift in a supportive situation.

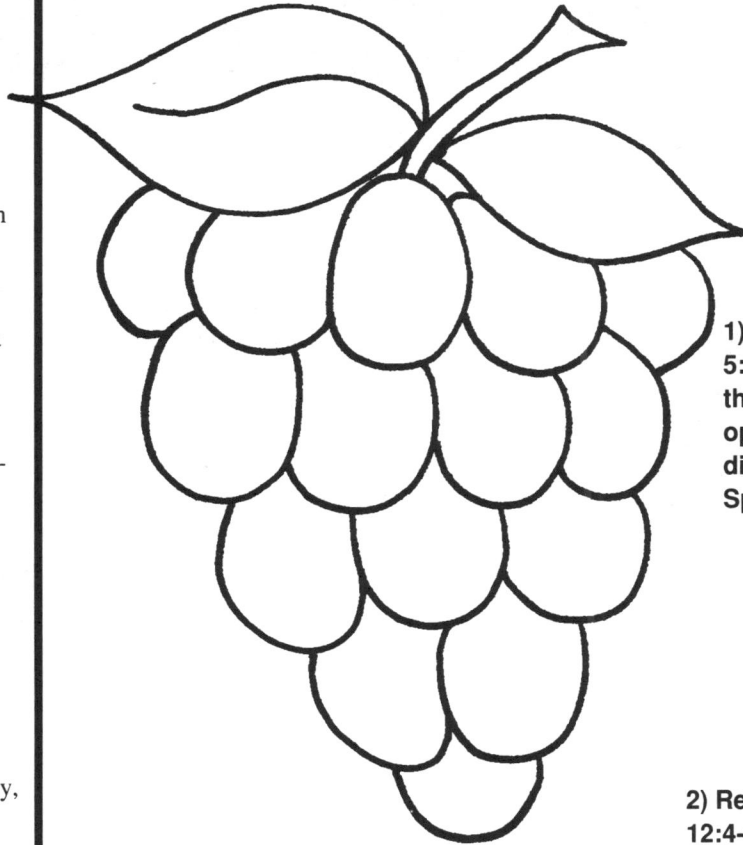

THE HOLY SPIRIT

1) Read Galatians 5:22-26 and write on the bunch of grapes opposite what the different 'fruit of the Spirit' are.

2) Read 1 Corinthians 12:4-11 and write one of the gifts of the Spirit on the boxes below.

♥ ♥ ♥ *Don't forget!* ♥ ♥ ♥

'I may speak in different languages of people or even angels. But if I do not have love, I am only a noisy bell or a crashing cymbal. I may have the gift of prophecy. I may understand all the secret things of God and have all knowledge, and I may have faith so great that I can move mountains. But even with all these things, if I do not have love, then I am nothing' (1 Corinthians 13:1-2).

WE ARE FAMILY

MEETING AIM:

To teach that the church is a 'family' of believers, and to encourage involvement in and attendance at church services.

MEETING PREPARATION

Recruit some church members to come to your youth group/club meeting to act as 'welcomers' and 'guides' to the church building. Brief these people thoroughly beforehand so they know what you want of them. Contact the church leaders for permission to use the main church building/sanctuary. Also ask them if the youth group/club can take part in some of or take a whole meeting.

WELCOME TO THE FAMILY
(10 mins)

Hold this meeting in your church building (most groups/clubs meet in a separate hall, room or home). Arrange for church members to be at the door to welcome the young people as they arrive and then mingle with them. You might want to have some light refreshments available to encourage a relaxed atmosphere.

Have a cassette player on hand repeatedly playing 'We are Family' by Sister Sledge as the young people arrive, or even better put this through the church PA (if you have one).

CHURCH TOUR (10-15 mins)

Get the church members to take small groups of young people (maximum six) on a guided tour of the inside and outside of your church building. Obviously some churches have more historical interest than others, but concentrate on explaining why the pulpit, altar/communion table, baptistery/font are in the places they are. Usually one of these components is in the most dominant geographical position. This links to the theology of your church (ie, churches that put great emphasis on the preaching of scripture usually have the pulpit in the most commanding position). Encourage questions and feedback.

Bring everyone back together and ask them to describe the 'vibes' that the church building gives them (eg, warm, homely, creepy, ancient).

SAY: 'People often gauge their opinion of a church by the look of the building, but is that what the church actually is? Later we will look at what a church is and should be, but first a game...'

EVERY SECOND COUNTS
(10 mins)

This version of the TV gameshow *Every Second Counts* is a bit of fun and illustrates the large number of local churches mentioned in the New Testament. Ideally the quiz master should be male, middle-aged, vertically challenged and balding - in other words, look like Paul Daniels.

Four contestants take it in turns to respond to a possible name of a New Testament church, announced by the quiz master with either - *'It's a fellowship, Paul'* - *(if they think the name is genuine)*,

OR

'It's a figment, Paul' - *(if they think it isn't)*.

The four contestants answer in turn. If they answer correctly they stay in the game, score a point and the next question goes to the next contestant - and so on. When a contestant gets an answer wrong they drop out. (Drape a tea towel over their head.)

The last contestant left wins - carrying on as long as they keep getting the answers right, or until you run out of church names.

Mix up the two lists of genuine and fictitious churches below.

'FELLOWSHIP'	'FICTION'
Athens *(Acts 17:16f)*	**Agamemnon**
Antioch *(Acts 13:1)*	**Epiglottis**
Berea *(Acts 17:10f)*	**Dettol**
Corinth *(1 Corinthians 1:2)*	**Ibiza**
Ephesus *(Ephesians 1:1)*	**Iota**
Troas *(Acts 20:5f)*	**Troy**
Sardis *(Revelation 3:1)*	**Tardis**
Philippi *(Philippians 1:1)*	**Trolop**
Azotus *(Acts 8:40)*	**Serdar**
Sharon *(Acts 9:35f)*	**Tracey**
Derbe *(Acts 14:6)*	**Epsom**
Rome *(Romans 1:7)*	**Moscow**
Thyatira *(Revelation 2:18)*	**Thyroid**
Syracuse *(Acts 28:12)*	**Smirnoff**
Malta *(Acts 28:1)*	**Majorca**
Sidon *(Acts 27:3)*	**Leadon**
Philadelphia *(Revelation 3:7)*	**Manitoba**
Perga *(Acts 13:13)*	**Chronicula**
Rhegium *(Acts 28:13)*	**Sydium**

THE FIRST CHURCH (15 mins)

SAY: 'Let's read about the first ever church to see how it worshipped together and attracted new believers.'

READ OUT LOUD: Acts 2:36-47. Explain that the first church didn't have its own building, but met in the Jewish temple or in each others' homes. There are still churches today which meet in homes or rented rooms/buildings/school halls. They lived together like a large extended family, sharing things and caring for each other.

Then as Christianity spread, more and more communities of believers or churches started up. So instead of one church which met in Jerusalem, there were churches in lots of other towns and cities.

DISCUSS: What marked out the first Christians as different from other people? Why is it that each Christian church is slightly different? What are the similarities and differences between the description of the first church and this church? What similarities are there between a church and a family?

SPOT THE CHRISTIAN
(10 mins)

Hand out a copy of the worksheet opposite to each individual. Give them three minutes to complete the sheet and then compare answers.

SAY: 'Many people have a mental picture of a Christian as being someone who is old or a bit out of date. The fact is that every single person opposite could be a Christian! The church is made up of all sorts of different people.'

CHURCH PLUG (15 mins)

Divide into small groups of three and ask each group to devise a 30-second TV advert about the church. The ad should include details about what the church is like, particular services/meetings of interest to various types of people, and above all 'sell' the church to the viewer. Give the groups 10 minutes to devise their ad which can be acted, sung (using a jingle), read, use captions or slogans etc. Then get each group in turn to perform their ad to the rest.

Discuss which ad was the most truthful, the most appealing, the most entertaining, etc. Pick up on some of the statements and slogans to delve into the young people's opinions and observations of church.

It could be good to get the adult 'welcomers' to stay and take part in this exercise and to compare their ad with the young people's. This could illustrate the different things people look for in a church.

FAMILY GET-TOGETHERS
(5 mins)

Read Hebrews 10:24-25 and then invite the young people to a suitable service. Ideally it should include them, hence the request to the church leaders for input from your group.

SPOT THE CHRISTIAN!

1

2

3

4

5

6

Which two people look MOST likely to be Christians?

No. ....

Why? ....
....
....
....
....
....

No. ....

Why? ....
....
....
....
....
....

Which two people look LEAST likely to be Christians?

No. ....

Why? ....
....
....
....
....
....

No. ....

Why? ....
....
....
....
....

WORLD BEST-SELLER

MEETING AIM:
To discover individuals' views and beliefs about the Bible. To begin to challenge popular misconceptions, stimulate interest in and explain the importance of reading scripture.

BLIND COOKING (10 mins)

You will need the following props to run this crowdbreaker: 2 liquidisers, 2 bananas, one pint of milk, two teaspoons of lemon juice, 2oz of ground almonds, two glace cherries, 20ml of single cream, 30ml of treacle, two sardine/anchovy or sild, two slices of cucumber, 2oz of semi-crushed flake chocolate, two straws, plus two bottles each of the following sauces: chocolate, strawberry, caramel/toffee, cherry.

Divide the ingredients/props into two identical selections on a large table. Plug the liquidisers into an electric socket. Ensure that anyone using this has clear instructions on its safe and proper use. This avoids accidents and mess!

Explain to the young people that the opening activity is a contest to discover who can make the most delicious milkshake. Get two volunteer makers/tasters. Explain that two lots of identical ingredients to choose from are laid out on the table.

Once the two volunteers come forward, explain that you only have one recipe card with instructions on how to make a delicious bananachoc milkshake. Toss a coin to decide which person gets the recipe card. To the person that loses, explain that apart from milk and a banana they may as well choose the other ingredients with a blindfold on since they don't know the recipe. Then quickly blindfold the person and guide them along their ingredients from which they choose six elements. Once selected take the blindfold off and give both contestants up to two minutes to blend and whisk a tasty milkshake.

Encourage both contestants to sip some of their creation and then hand it round the group for anyone else brave or thirsty enough to try some!

At the end make the point that one contestant had a large advantage because they had the recipe which gave them expert advice on the right combination to make the best possible use of the ingredients. Introduce today's theme by saying that you believe it is possible to have a similar advantage in life by using the maker's instructions for living. If he made us and wrote a recipe book for living the best way, it must be worth checking out!

BANANA-CHOC MILKSHAKE RECIPE

Blend a peeled banana and one teaspoon of lemon juice for 15 seconds. Add ½ pint milk, 10ml of cream and a dessert spoon of chocolate sauce. Blend together for 30 seconds and pour into a tall glass. Cut a line from the centre of a slice of cucumber to the edge, then put the slice over the lip of the glass. Crumble a small amount of crushed chocolate flake onto the froth of the shake and it's ready to drink with a straw!

IN OR OUT (10 mins)

Many people misquote the Bible. Dot Cotton who used to appear in the BBC soap *Eastenders* was always mangling and misquoting scripture. Read out the quotes below and at the same time put the quote on a card or OHP. Allow three second's thinking time, then ask everyone to shout 'in' if they think it is a genuine quote from scripture, or 'out' if they think it isn't.

1) In the beginning God created the sky and the earth - **IN** *(Genesis 1:1)*
2) God helps those who help themselves - **OUT**
3) Cleanliness is next to godliness - **OUT**
4) You must not steal - **IN** *(Exodus 20:15)*
5) There is a time for everything - **IN** *(Ecclesiastes 3:1)*
6) Everyone is equal under the sun - **OUT**
7) Father forgive them, because they don't know what they are doing - **IN** *(Luke 23:34)*
8) For what we are about to receive may the Lord make us truly thankful - **OUT**
9) Money is the root of all evil - **OUT** ('the love of money' is described as the root of all evil in *1 Timothy 6:10*)
10) Hell hath no fury like a woman scorned - **OUT** (Shakespeare, not scripture!)
11) Don't judge other people, or you will be judged - **IN** *(Matthew 7:1)*
12) Turn or burn - **OUT**
13) Do all you can to lead a peaceful life - **IN** *(1 Thessalonians 4:11)*
14) He who would valiant be, against all disaster - **OUT** (popular school hymn written by John Bunyan)
15) Do not be fooled: you can't cheat God - **IN** *(Galatians 6:7)*

20 QUESTIONS (20+ mins)

Hand out photocopies of the 20 Questions tick sheet (opposite) and a pen/pencil. Allow up to five minutes for the sheets to be completed by individuals. Then comes the tricky part!

As the group share their answers it is important to allow people to have their own views but at the same time ask appropriate questions to get behind the reasons why they answered as they did. This applies just as much to Christians who gave very 'positive' answers.

Carefully prepare questions beforehand that will get people talking and discussing their answers. Use *Why, When, How, If* type questions that cannot be answered by a simple 'yes' or 'no'.

Note that questions 11 to 16 are illustrated by the selected readings listed at the end of the 'Right Riveting Read' section.

RIGHT RIVETING READ (20 mins)

Select a member of the group, one of the leaders or a member of the church congregation to talk for a maximum of five minutes about their favourite passage/story from scripture. They need to say why it's their favourite and how it has spoken to/challenged/encouraged/surprised them. And of course, they should also read out the passage (from a modern translation), up to a maximum of 20 verses.

Then ask the young people what their favourite 'bits' from the Bible are and why.

Explain that the word 'Bible' comes from the Greek word *biblia* meaning 'books', and that this collection of 66 books took many different people over 1,000 years to write.

Conclude this session by reading out the following verses from the Bible, some of which will be familiar to them, others may surprise:

'The Lord is my shepherd; I have everything I need' *Psalm 23:1,* (famous poetry).

'When the Levite got home, he took a knife and cut his slave woman into twelve parts, limb by limb. Then he sent a part to each part of Israel' *Judges 19:29,* (historical accounts of lawless frontier days of Old Testament Israel).

'My lover's left arm is under my head, and his right arm holds me tight' *Song of Solomon 8:3,* (song celebrating sexual love).

'If you loudly greet your neighbour early in the morning, he will think of it as a curse' *Proverbs 27:14*, (practical tips on living).

'Whoever says that he lives in God must live as Jesus lived' *1 John 2:6*, (a call to a radical alternative lifestyle).

'God loved the world so much that he gave his one and only Son so that whoever believes in him may not be lost, but have eternal life' *John 3:16*, (the main theme of the Bible: God's plan to save the human race from sin and death through Jesus Christ).

CRUCIAL READING (5 mins)

Read 2 Timothy 3:14-17, then say: 'This part of the Bible was written by St Paul to his friend Timothy to encourage him in his Christian faith. Timothy had learned about Jesus from childhood. Paul explains why he thinks reading the scriptures is so important - because it is inspired by God and is more than just a good read or wise sayings, but actually a guidebook for living from God himself.'

Display a range of modern translations/paraphrases of the Bible for your group to look at. As well as different translations, also have some of the newer editions available which are specifically aimed at young people. These Bibles include useful 'helps' and notes which make them an excellent buy.

Particularly recommended are: [NIV] The Insight Bible (Hodders); [Living Bible] The Student Bible (Kingsway); and [New Century Version] The Youth Bible (Word), which in its paperback format is the only Bible I have seen with the word 'sex' on the front cover!

OPTIONAL EXTRAS

BIBLE TRIVIA GAME

There are a host of different Bible trivia games available. Your local Christian bookshop will stock a range, or you may find someone in your church would lend you theirs. If your group have a fairly good level of Bible knowledge a Bible Trivial Pursuits evening will be both fun and instructive. Alternatively, for groups with less Bible knowledge, you could write your own questions geared to them. These could be based on the teaching content in the group over the past few weeks/term/year.

Scriptures quoted from The Youth Bible, New Century Version (Anglicised Edition) © 1993 by Nelson Word Ltd, 9 Holdom Ave, Bletchley, Milton Keynes MK1 1QR.

20 Questions

Give your honest opinions to the following statements by ticking either the 'Agree' (A) or 'Disagree' (D) boxes.

A D

1) The Bible is always lots of fun to read
2) The Bible is sometimes interesting, but sometimes boring
3) The Bible is totally boring and there is no point in reading it anyway
4) The Bible is hard to understand
5) The Bible is written in really old-fashioned language
6) I try to read the Bible at least once a week
7) I try to read the Bible at least three times a week
8) I never have time to read the Bible
9) I don't see how the Bible has anything to do with life today
10) The Bible is full of rules and regulations
11) The Bible contains some of the world's most famous poetry
12) The Bible contains gory and violent stories
13) The Bible contains a song which celebrates sexual love
14) The Bible contains practical and helpful tips on living
15) The Bible suggests a radical alternative lifestyle
16) The main theme of the Bible is Jesus and God's plan to save humankind from the power of sin and death
17) Science has proved that the Bible is full of mistakes
18) I would prefer someone else explain the Bible to me than try to read it for myself
19) The Bible contains contradictions
20) Although I sometimes fail, I try to live my life according to what the Bible says

PHOTO: JIM LORING

PRAYER

MEETING AIM:
To teach that prayer is natural and makes a difference. Also to encourage the group to actually pray out loud.

NATURAL OR UNNATURAL?
(15 mins)
Hand out pens and a sheet of A5 paper to everyone. Ask them to write the word 'natural' at the top of one side of the page, and the word 'unnatural' at the top of the other side. Then ask the group to compile a list of things they regard as natural, eg laughter, thirst; and unnatural, eg exhaust fumes, plastic flowers.

Allow five minutes and then ask for people to read out their lists. Use a flip chart or write on an OHP to compile a master list. Allow some discussion/debate over controversial or questionable entries.

It may be that some people have suggested some God-aware/religious qualities on their 'natural' list. Conclude this section by saying that many people would regard prayer as a natural element, not least because it is something that everyone does at some stage in their life. When new people groups have been 'discovered' by Western civilisation, the people/tribe always have a god or gods which they attempted to communicate with. This in a nutshell is what prayer is - communicating with God.

TALK AND LISTEN (10 mins)
Divide the group into pairs. One person is the talker, the other is the listener. Get the talkers to stand on one side of the room, with the listeners standing opposite their partner on the other side of the room.

Listeners each receive a pad of paper and a pen and are told to write down word for word what the talker says.

The talkers are each given a different book (it can be anything from a DIY manual to a technical text book; a best-selling novel to a biography). Ask them to open the book at random and start reading at a slow enough pace for the listeners to write down what they say.

If you have less fewer than five pairs, switch on a radio which is tuned in to a speech programme, eg, BBC Radio 4. This will add some distracting background interference, making the listener's job more difficult. If you have five pairs or more, the hubbub from all those raised voices will be distracting enough without additional interference.

After about three minutes of mayhem, call things to a halt. Then get the listeners to read back to the talkers what they recorded. Pick out one or two to be read out to everyone, highlighting the errors and misheard elements of the message.

Conclude this exercise by saying that communication is a tricky business. What we say to someone can be misheard or misunderstood. But what about when we try to communicate with God, or God tries to communicate with us? This process can be just as difficult sometimes.

ASK: What sort of things provide the interference when we try to pray to God? What stops us from praying? How can God possibly understand all the different prayer messages that he must get each minute of the day? What can stop us hearing right from God?

SWEDISH BIBLE STUDY
(20 mins)
Use the Swedish Bible study method to examine Jesus' teaching on prayer. For this you will need to photocopy the card with symbols below. Enlarge the image by 100%.

As a group read together Luke 11:1-13, then hand out a card and pen to everyone. Explain that they need to go over the passage and next to each symbol do the following:
■ Beside the arrow pointing upwards write something these verses teach us about Jesus/God.
■ Beside the arrow pointing downwards write something these verses teach about humankind.
■ Beside the lightbulb write some new insight or discovery you have made from reading these verses.

⬆
⬇
💡
!
?
➡

■ Beside the exclamation mark write what is the most exciting verse in your opinion and why.
■ Beside the question mark write anything you didn't understand or want to ask about.
■ Beside the arrow pointing sideways write down something which these verses say we should do.

N.B. *You may need to repeat these instructions several times. Also make sure everyone has access to a Bible.*

Allow 8-10 minutes for the Swedish Bible study, then ask for people to feedback. Ask for everyone's response to the first symbol before moving on to the next answer.

Emphasise that prayer can be hard work, but very rewarding, so we need to be persistent. You may want to give a short three-minute 'prayer changes things' talk with examples from your life of answered prayer, plus what you learned from situations where your prayer was not answered in the way you wanted/expected.

NEWSPRAYER (5 mins)
Conclude by splitting into small groups for the Prayer Diary exercise right, or alternatively show a video recording of that day's television news headlines, or select three or four headlines from the newspapers and photocopy them onto an OHP acetate or simply stick them on a cork board.

If you have a group which are anxious about praying out loud, ask them to write a prayer about one of the news subjects and then in turn read them out. Alternatively, get them in a circle and ask them to take turns to pray a one-sentence prayer.

PRAYER DIARY
Hand out copies of the prayer diary sheet opposite and ask people to get together in groups of three (this may need to be carefully overseen to ensure people are not left out - groups of two or four are acceptable, but not preferable).

Either at the meeting or in their own time, encourage the small groups to meet as prayer triplets at least once a week for 15 minutes, to list prayer needs and answers using the prayer diary sheet.

You could use this as part of your ongoing programme over the next few weeks.

Be sure to speak to at least one person from each small group over the next few weeks to encourage them to pray together.

Prayer Diary

Date	Prayer details	Date	Answer details

'Do not worry about anything, but pray and ask God for everything you need, always giving thanks' (Philippians 4:6).

'Pray in the spirit at all times with all kinds of prayers, asking for everything you need. To do this you must always be ready and never give up. Always pray for all God's people (Ephesians 6:18).

Date	Prayer details	Date	Answer details

'Pray for all rulers and for all who have authority' (1 Timothy 2:1-2).

FORGIVENESS

MEETING AIM:
To teach that God is willing to forgive us, but this is conditional on us forgiving others.

THE SIN BIN (15 mins)
Begin this session with a contact sports game such as uni-hock, basketball or 5-a-side soccer. At the first foul blow a whistle to stop the game and tell the person who committed the foul to apologise. Then ask the person who was fouled if he/she accepts the apology. If they say 'yes', award them a free kick/hit/shot. If they say 'no', as well as awarding the free kick/hit/shot, take out a red card and order the player who committed the foul off to the 'sin bin' for 5 minutes/or the rest of the game.

Explain to the person who committed the offence that you are doing this because the other player refused to accept his/her apology.

Once the first player gets sent off in this way, the other players are likely to continue to refuse to apologise when they get fouled and the game will descend into farce with less and less players left actually playing, and most on the sidelines.

At the end of the game, explain that the theme this week is forgiveness. Point out that a lack of forgiveness in the game removed the purpose and pleasure of the game, once the initial humour of the situation was gone.

IS SORRY ENOUGH? (25 mins)
Hand everyone a photocopy of the sheet opposite. Read out the story of Kirsty and Amber and allow up to 5 minutes for people to write their response. Then get the group to read out their answers. Without taking sides, stimulate a discussion on the issue of forgiveness. Develop the arguments raised and take people's reactions further (eg

Kirsty's justifiable anger may result in the end of a friendship, which in the long term could hurt Kirsty as much or more than Amber).

Encourage your young people to draw on personal examples of friends breaking promises and falling out or making up. Many young people go through this process on a regular basis, so you may find that 25 minutes is nothing like enough time for this section.

NEWSPAPER BINGO (5 mins)
Divide your group into two or more equal teams (maximum four in a team). Give each group a pile of newspapers (minimum six per team), a pen and a newspaper bingo card (see example below). You could make up your own card if you prefer. The winning team is the one which can rip out of its papers stories which have examples of all of the categories on the bingo card. If at the end of five minutes no team has shouted 'full house', the winner is the team with most categories ticked.

At the end of the game make the point that our newspapers are full of stories of people who have been wronged by others. When we are wronged, once we get over the initial shock/pain we are faced with a choice: to bear a grudge and become bitter about that person, or to forgive them and begin to put it behind us.

Ask: Why is it often hard to forgive?

FORGIVE US AS WE FORGIVE OTHERS (10+ mins)
Read 1 Timothy 1:12-17 then briefly explain how Paul had persecuted the early Christians until he was dramatically confronted by the power and reality of the risen Christ. He then became a follower of Jesus and went to those he formerly persecuted to work with

and alongside them to spread the gospel.

Paul had to say 'sorry' to God and the Christians. The Christians could have rejected his apology and not allowed Paul any contact with them, but they chose to forgive him. Underline that the history of the church would have been crucially different if the early Christians had rejected Paul the new convert who wanted forgiveness.

Play some appropriate music on a cassette player or sing some worship songs which focus on the theme of forgiveness and getting right with God.

During this time ask the group to consider carefully whether there is a person or situation in which they need to ask God (and others) for forgiveness. Also ask them to consider whether they are holding a grudge against someone who has wronged them. Stress that Jesus taught that if we fail to forgive others, God cannot forgive us. It may be appropriate to pray together the Lord's Prayer at this point - using it as a vehicle to ask God's forgiveness and to forgive others.

Encourage members within the group to get right with each other there and then or as soon as possible.

OPTIONAL EXTRAS

THE HIDING PLACE
Show part or all of the film 'The Hiding Place', the true story of Corrie ten Boom and her family who sheltered Jews in occupied Holland during World War II. When Corrie and her sister were sent to a concentration camp, their Christian faith and ability to forgive the evil camp wardens were stretched to the limit. This feature length video is available for sale or rent from many Christian bookshops, or in case of difficulty contact: International Films, c/o Scripture Press, Raans Road, Amersham, Bucks HP6 6JQ. Tel: 0494 722151.

NEWSPAPER BINGO

Adultery	Murder	Slander	Racism
Fraud/Cheating	Broken promise	Unkind act	Sexism
Thoughtlessness	Sexual crime	Burglary	Cruelty

IS SORRY ENOUGH?

Amber and Kirsty had been best friends for over a year. They got on so well and had such a similar attitude to life that many people thought they must be twins. They had the same taste in clothes, boys and music. In particular they both liked 'The Grifters' who had just announced the dates for their European tour.

Amber and Kirsty had been listening to The Grifters for ages, even before they had become a well-known band. They had all their albums and had been making plans to buy tickets at the one and only British concert date for the latest Grifters tour. It meant a very early start to catch the 5.48am train to get to town early enough to be sure of a ticket when they went on sale at 9am.

On the big day, Kirsty was at the station by 5.30, but by 5.45 there was still no sign of Amber. As the train arrived at the station Kirsty frantically ran out of the entrance to see if her friend was running up the road, but there was no sign of her. Kirsty turned round in time to see the train leaving the platform - now she had missed the train too!

According to the timetable there wasn't another train for an hour, so Kirsty walked to Amber's house a mile away and knocked on the door. It took ages for anyone to answer, and then when the door opened it was Amber's dad. He wasn't too pleased at being woken up early.

Amber eventually opened her bedroom door. 'I thought we agreed to meet at the station in time for the first train,' said an angry Kirsty.

'Oh sorry, I must've overslept,' said Amber. But Kirsty didn't think she looked very sorry.

'If you got there on time you should have caught the train without me,' said Amber. 'Oh well, if you catch the next train you can still get there before the ticket office opens. Get an extra ticket for me, will you?' she added.

Kirsty hit the roof and started shouting at Amber about breaking her promise and how she could buy her own ticket. Amber yawned and apologised again while rubbing her eyes. Kirsty stormed out of the house.

Although Kirsty caught the 6.48 train, by the time she got to the ticket office at 8.30 the queue was enormous. At about 10am it started to rain. At 11.15 the queue had progressed so that Kirsty had only about 30 people in front of her. By then she had decided to buy only one ticket. It would serve Amber right!

Then a man announced that all the tickets were sold, so could everyone please leave?

Without a ticket and having wasted a whole morning and the price of the train fare; having got wet and cold, and worst of all been let down by her friend, Kirsty felt miserable on the journey home. As she sat on the train she thought about Amber, her so-called friend. They were supposed to be meeting up tomorrow to go shopping. Then on Monday they normally walked to school together. Amber had said 'sorry' twice, but was that enough?

● Write down how you think Kirsty should react to this situation. Give reasons for your answer.

❓ DOUBTS ❓

MEETING AIM:

To recognise that doubt is not necessarily shameful, but can be a positive force for growth in the Christian life. Also that doubts come from several sources, that they shouldn't frighten us - our God has the answers.

STARTER OPTIONS

Here are two attention-grabbing ways to start the evening:

1. Start with a fairly boring, lengthy, spoken introduction. Suddenly a stranger crashes through the door, points a starting pistol at you, shoots and runs off. When people have calmed down again, ask them to write a description of the stranger. They saw him - but because the experience was so out of the ordinary, a lot of their ideas will be extremely unclear. Just like becoming a Christian, really.

2. When people arrive, the place is locked and in darkness. Have you forgotten to turn up? Is it the wrong night? Has it been cancelled? Keep them hanging about until they've almost decided to give up and go home. Then let them in - but use the experience to launch a discussion of how it feels to be in a state of doubt about what's going on...

INSTANT VOTE (5 mins)

Ask people to respond to each of these statements. If they are absolutely convinced that they are true, they should stand up and cheer loudly. If they are undecided, they should sit still and scratch their heads, and if they are pretty sure the statement is false, they should lean forward, scowl and shake their heads slowly.

1) Edinburgh is further north than Moscow.
2) Manchester United will win the European Cup.
3) The next total eclipse of the sun occurs in Britain during 1996.
4) There is life on other planets.
5) The earliest-surviving cigarette packet dates from 1860.
6) The capital city of Mongolia is called Mongo.
7) Billy Graham's middle name is Franklin.
8) The youth leader is a complete idiot.
9) The Body Shop never advertises.
10) Tomorrow something great is going to happen.

(1,5,7 and 9 are all correct.)

Analyse what happened. There are different reasons for uncertainty: because you don't know the facts; because nobody knows; or because it's a matter of opinion. Why do Christians sometimes find themselves uncertain about their faith?

DIAGNOSIS (15 mins)

The first thing is to establish what we know about doubts. Divide into three groups. Ask one to answer the *difficult questions* which often cause doubts (eg: Can you trust the Bible? Did the resurrection happen?).

Another should list the *puzzling circumstances* which cause doubts (eg why your girlfriend is dying of cancer; when your prayers aren't being answered). Ask the third to list the *personal causes* there can be (eg feeling let down by Christians; feeling discouraged by the power of temptation).

Check the lists and discuss:
1) Which of these, in your experience is the biggest problem of all?
2) Do doubts start suddenly or grow over a period of time?
3) Are these causes of doubt all separate, or do they ever overlap?

Then say: 'Human beings aren't just bodies, and aren't just minds. Spirit, soul and body are all interlinked, so when doubts come, they won't always be rational, logical, intellectual problems. Their strength may derive from damaged emotions or a weakened body.'

Paul Little in his book, *How To Give Away Your Faith* (IVP), claims that most people can come up with only seven basic objections to the Christian faith - and there are answers to all of them! So we shouldn't be worried that Christianity will let us down intellectually. Doubts aren't fatal.

POSITIVE AND NEGATIVE (15 mins)

Play a game in two teams. One team ties a piece of red wool on each member's left arm; the other team uses blue. People run around and the blues try to pull off the red armbands within a five-minute limit. The reds are allowed to take evasive action, but must not fight back or remove the blue armbands.

Then play the game again with a difference. This time both teams are trying to pull off the other's armbands within the five-minute limit.

Discuss how different it felt playing the second way - especially for the reds! You're much more likely to do well if you can positively go on the attack, instead of just negatively running away.

Explain that this applies to our doubts too. Many people react negatively when they have doubts - they stuff them down into their subconscious and try to forget them (like the blue team!) they don't go away - they just press harder. Positive doubting means dragging your feelings out into the open and looking at them fearlessly. Why are you doubting? What's the state of the evidence? Are there answers to your questions you haven't explored?

GREAT BIBLICAL DOUBTERS (20 mins)

Hand out copies of the report sheets (opposite) and work through the biblical passages, filling it in. Feedback, then make the points:
1) Some of God's greatest servants had doubts - to doubt God isn't shameful or immature.
2) There are obvious causes for the doubts in each case. These things are recorded so that we will be warned!
3) God doesn't condemn his doubting servants, but he does supply answers to help them.

WRAP UP (5 mins)

Give people a moment to think about (maybe even write down) the three biggest doubt-producers in their own lives. When they have their list, let them think through what action they need to take to deal with them positively rather than letting them fester negatively. Finally, stress again the main points you've made on the way through, and end by praying together.

OPTIONAL EXTRAS

Many young Christians have never seriously examined the basis of their faith. Have some good short books and booklets available on the spot for them to borrow afterwards, to look at the evidence for Christian belief.

Particularly recommended is *Good Questions* - a cassette or video by Steve Chalke (Scripture Union), and *It Makes Sense* by Stephen Gaukroger (Scripture Union).

NAME	UNDERLYING REASON FOR DOUBTS	WHAT DID THIS PERSON DOUBT?	WHAT HAPPENED?
ELIJAH 1 Kings 19:3-18			
THOMAS John 20:24-29			
GIDEON Judges 6:1-16			
AARON Exodus 32:1-9			

Book Two: Lifestyle

Most of us are not aware of the decisions we make to behave as we do. But young people are actually in the process of making those decisions. As they progress into independence and responsibility, who and what will guide their thinking?

The following programme ideas open up some of the issues that fill young people's minds day in and day out: questions of self-esteem, money, sex, honesty. Don't be tempted to preach this term: instead be prepared to listen, to ask questions, to provide a non-judgemental arena in which your young people can take a long hard look at themselves and their lifestyle, and see how they measure up to God's plans for them.

READY-TO-USE-MEETING GUIDE

PUBLICITY PAGE

Get your meeting noticed by using the ready-to-photocopy artwork below to promote the first week of this term-long series of meetings. Simply add the details of venue and time and photocopy onto paper or thin coloured card. This image can be shrunk in size to use as a personal invite or expanded to poster size to pin onto a notice board at church, school, youth club etc.

LIFE • SEIZE THE DAY • FLUNK

BE UNIQUE • RESIST THE SYSTEM • DON'T CONFORM •

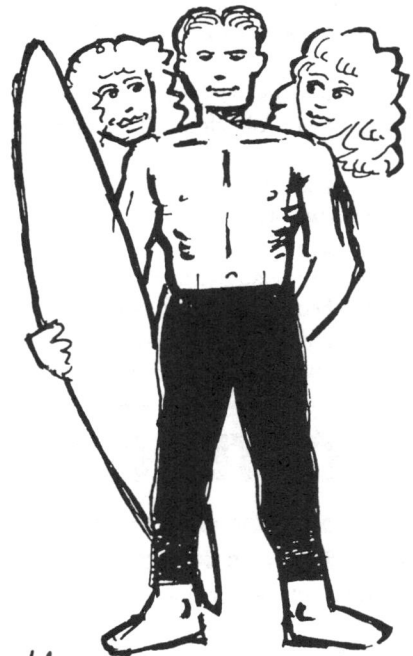

GOODBYE • THINK • THINK • THINK • DON'T

REBELL!ON

DESIGNER

1

OF THE CR?WD

B ALL U

WERE CREATED 2 B •

FIGHT APATHY • KISS

JOIN US

THINK 4 YOURSELF B • ALIVE

PRESSURE

MEETING AIM:

To help young people identify both positive and negative pressures that affect their lives, and to suggest practical ways to resist the pressure to conform to unbiblical standards.

STANDING HIGH JUMP
(10 mins)

For this simple standing high jump game you need one or two old mattresses, several long strips of cloth, and three long bamboo canes (at least 150cm). On two of the canes make a series of pen marks, the first 15cm from the end of the cane, then in 5cm spaces.

Two leaders each hold one of the marked canes upright from the ground, with the third cane acting as a horizontal bar over which everyone must jump. Start at the 15cm mark and increase the height by 5cm each round. Put the mattresses on the landing side of the bar and encourage people to make acrobatic jumps!

The young people line up with their ankles bound together by the old cloths. If anyone touches the bar as they jump, they are out of the game. Continue increasing the height until you have a winner.

Conclude by saying: 'No matter how good we are at jumping, we all eventually failed to jump the bar because of the pressure of gravity which pulls us down to earth.

'This week we will check out some of the pressures that affect us. Some of these pressures are good and positive and helpful, and some of these pressures are bad and negative, even dangerous.'

HELP OR HINDRANCE?
(10 mins)

Photocopy onto an OHP acetate the news story below, then project it onto a wall/screen and read it to the whole group.

Then ask the group:
1) What qualifications and qualities should an agony aunt/uncle have?
2) Is it a good thing or a bad thing that most teens take a lot of advice from TV and magazines?
3) Who do you wish gave more advice on drugs, sex, relationships, careers, lifestyle, morals etc?
Parents/church/media 'experts'/teachers?

PRESSURE POINTS
(20-25 mins)

Put everyone into groups of three. They will need a Bible each, and one pressure points worksheet and a pen. Allow 10-15 minutes for them to complete the worksheet. Make sure you are available if any of the small groups are struggling or have questions. Then get everyone back together to feed back their answers and opinions. Be sure to have completed this mini Bible study yourself beforehand.

WHO INFLUENCES YOU MOST? (up to 10 mins)

Hand out photocopies of the 'Who Influences You Most?' questionnaire, and give them three minutes to complete it. Then invite people to feed back if they want to. You may find this exercise very informative and possibly surprising.

IT HAPPENED TO ME (10 mins)

Get the young people into groups of three. Then ask each group member to share a time when they felt their friends strongly influenced or pressurised them into doing something they didn't want to do, or knew was wrong. Feed back comments and pick up on common experiences.

Then ask the groups to decide which of the following suggestions is the best way to resist negative pressure.

- Simply say 'no'.
- Make up an excuse.
- Say: 'This is against my beliefs'.
- Suggest another idea/activity.
- Walk away.
- Say: 'This is wrong and I'm not doing it'.
- Other: ....

'90% OF TEENS GET SEX & DRUGS ADVICE FROM MEDIA'

More than 90% of 14 and 15-year-olds rely on the media to give them most of the facts on sex, drugs and HIV, according to a recent YMCA survey.

The research, carried out by Hove YMCA, into 600 14 to 25-year-olds in the town found that 91% of 14 to 15-year-old girls questioned gleaned much of their information from magazines, while 92% of boys the same age learned about life from the TV.

Overall, the young people expressed an overwhelming need for advice on HIV, pregnancy, sex, drugs and careers.

The YMCA survey was released the same week that a Health Education Authority (HEA) sex guide for teenagers was withdrawn just days before it was to go on sale.

Your Pocket Guide to Sex was written by Nick Fisher, agony uncle for Just 17 magazine, but was branded as 'distasteful and smutty' by the then health minister Dr Brian Mawhinney. A committed Christian and vice-president of Crusaders, Mawhinney 'strongly advised' the Government-funded HEA to pulp the book.

The Archbishop of Canterbury denounced publicly-funded bodies for apparently encouraging the idea among young people that sex was just another consumer pleasure.

He told an AIDS conference in London recently: 'Saying "no" to the attractions of promiscuous relationships is a way of behaviour within the reach of us all.'

He went on to criticise the promotion of a 'condom culture'.

He told delegates that while there were no easy answers when it came to sex education, 'the secular approach sometimes makes it easy by sweeping all standards away, but the long-term consequences are dire indeed'.

The Department of Health insisted no public funds had been used to produce *Your Pocket Guide to Sex*. The author, 34-year-old Nick Fisher, said in a *Daily Mail* article in 1993 that he lost his virginity aged 13 to another 13-year-old while on holiday.

In the article he admitted his teens were 'somewhat of a disaster. I fought with my parents and got expelled from school. I was a very obnoxious, precocious boy. I thought I knew everything.'

According to the *Daily Mail* Fisher's first marriage at 26 ended in divorce.

PRESSURE POINTS

Check out these situations from the Bible of various people under pressure to do something they don't want to do. What can we learn from their successes and failures?

MOSES
READ *Exodus 1:22-2:10* and *Hebrews 11:24-26.*

List the temptations/pressures on Moses to stay with his adopted Egyptian family instead of identify himself as a Hebrew.

....
....
....
....
....
....

PETER
READ *Matthew 26:69-75.*

What advice would you give Peter to resist the pressure of a similar situation?

....
....
....
....
....
....

JESUS
READ *Matthew 4:1-11.*

Can you identify what strategies Jesus used to resist the tempting pressure of Satan? List them.

....
....
....
....
....
....

WHO INFLUENCES YOU MOST?

This exercise should show you who influences you the most. Next to each action, eg buying clothes, list in the appropriate column whether your parent(s), friends, media etc influence the decision you make. If they influence you a lot in that category draw a ✳. If they influence you a little draw a +, if they do not influence you leave the square blank. You are only allowed to draw one ✳ and up to three + per category.

In what ways do they influence you?	parent(s)	friends	media (films, TV, adverts, magazines)	brother/ sister	uncle/ aunt/ grandad/ grandma	youth worker/ leader	teacher
buying clothes							
choosing a hairstyle							
say 'yes' or 'no' to taking drugs							
say 'yes' or 'no' to smoking							
say 'yes' or 'no' to drinking alcohol							
say 'yes' or 'no' to sex							
say 'yes' or 'no' to shoplifting							
participating in sports							
going to church							
swearing							
what I eat							
listening to music							
lying							
going to the cinema							
going to night club/rave							

THE REAL YOU

MEETING AIM:

Many young people have a low self-esteem. This meeting aims to show that what we believe about how and why we were created affects the way we value or devalue ourselves. It also underlines that God really likes us and that comparing ourselves to 'perfect' media images can be unhealthy.

SPOT THE CELEB (5-10 mins)

Buy a copy of TV Hits magazine or a similar magazine full of posters and pictures of 'celebrities'. Tear out between a dozen and 20 pictures, write a number in the corner of the picture and blue-tak/sellotape them to the walls of the meeting venue.

As the young people arrive, hand out paper and pens and ask them to walk around the room identifying as many 'celebs' as they can. After reading out the answers, get the girls and then the fellers to vote for the best-looking of the celebs.

MIRROR MIME (5 mins)

Get everyone into pairs, mixed sex if possible. Assign one person 'A', the other 'B'. Ask them to face each other with toes almost touching. Ask the 'A's' to go through their morning routine at the bathroom sink in front of the mirror. They need to mime their regular habit of washing, brushing their teeth, gargling with mouthwash, applying make-up, shaving, applying deodorant, putting in contact lenses, squeezing zits or whatever! 'B' must imitate exactly all the movements made by their partner as though they were the mirror image. Then swop the roles so 'B' leads and 'A' copies.

Stop after five minutes and allow the group to talk, laugh and discuss their morning routine.

ASK: 'Do girls take more care about the way they look than boys?'

PERFECT PERSON IDENTIKIT (15 mins)

Hand out lots of glossy magazines, catalogues and teen magazines, scissors, glue and some A2-size card. In small groups of three to five ask them to cut out and create an identikit picture of the 'perfect' man and woman.

Display the pictures on the wall and ask the group to discuss:
● Common factors in the pictures, eg curvy figure and clear skin for the girls, and muscles and tan for the lads.
● Are most people happy with the way they

look or is there one feature that most people would like to change?
● How important are good looks?
● Do glossy images of 'perfect'-looking people in magazines make people more insecure/unhappy with the way they look?

NOSE JOB (25 mins)

Hand out copies of the sheet opposite for the group to complete individually. Allow up to 10 minutes, then share and discuss feelings for 15 minutes or so.

BOO HOO! (7 mins)

Ask for four volunteers (although two will suffice). If they are reluctant to come forward, tempt them with the prize. (If you have a limited budget it could be a packet of mints. If you have money to burn(!) buy some Lynx deodorant for the lads, and Impulse body spray for the girls.)

Each person is given a large onion (Spanish onions are the best for this) and told that they need to peel off the skins to reach the centre of the onion. The first person to do this wins. The only snag is they have to do this with their bare hands.

Have tissues, soap, water and towels available for the contestants to dry their eyes and clean up after the game. Don't forget the smelly prizes!

Then say: 'Some sociologists and philosophers think you and I are just like onions. They believe that humans are made by a series of influences and experiences. These are like the skins of an onion and they build up layer on layer to make up the people we are. So parents, teachers, friends, our environment, and a whole stack of other things, including the expectations of these people and the treatment we receive from them, make us who we are.

'These people say that if you peel away these layers, just like an onion, there is nothing left. People are just a product of these experiences and pressures from people and things.

'The Bible teaches that humans are more than just a hollow onion. It teaches that we have been created as unique people, in the image of God, and that a part of us will live on after we die.

'So although things and people do affect and influence us in major ways, we still have the ability to decide what to do. It is no use blaming all the bad things we do on our upbringing or our friends. We have to take responsibility for our own actions.

'The Bible teaches that we are more like a peach than an onion. A peach has a stone in its heart. Underneath the flesh and juice is something else, unseen from the outside. The stone is the unique heart of the peach.'

At this point hand out peaches, nectarines, apricots or nuts for everyone to eat (adapt the talk according to which fruit you use).

YOU'RE BEAUTIFUL! (5 mins)

Conclude by reading out this poem written by Pip Wilson. Read it slowly, allowing each line to sink in and take effect.

If You're Convinced There Is No God...
You are an accident,
You are a creation out of chaos,
You have no meaning, no reason for being here, You are worth nothing, unless you perform a use, or meet a need.
People may choose to value you for what you do because they need you or because they want you to value them in return.
You have no inherent value.
You are a human doing not a human being.
Your place of birth was accidental.
You have no purpose for life, except the one you give yourself.
Your only real achievement will be to reproduce, which is meaningless.
Your personality is a result of parents, friends and heroes. You are nothing special, unless you are famous.
You must earn your love, unless you choose to love yourself unconditionally.
No one else will. If you died tomorrow that would be your end. Finito.

But God Says...
You are a beautiful human being.
As you listen to these words, don't hear them flippantly. They are spoken for each one of you.
YOU are a valuable person.
YOU are a special person.
YOU are a unique person.
YOU are beautiful.
YOU are precious.
YOU are unrepeatable.
YOU are mysterious.
YOU are a beautiful human person.
No one will ever exist like you,
No one will ever experience a life that you have experienced.
You are so special and valuable that Jesus has died for you.
His love is completely and totally 100% for you. His love for you is unconditional.

© Pip Wilson

What would help Natasha feel better about herself?

(Tick up to three boxes)

- [ ] Tube of extra thick make-up
- [ ] A large brown paper bag
- [ ] To be told by a friend that she looks fine
- [ ] A new nose job
- [ ] Knowing God really loves her
- [ ] Becoming a backing singer with Barry Manilow
- [ ] A boyfriend
- [ ] Not reading any women's mags or watching TV ads

Read these verses from the NIV Bible, then answer the questions below:

'God created man in his own image... male and female he created them' (Genesis 1:27).

'For you created my inmost being; you knit me together in my mother's womb. I praise you because I am fearfully and wonderfully made' (Psalm 139:13-14).

'Don't you know that you yourselves are God's temple and that God's Spirit lives in you?' (1 Corinthians 3:16).

'We are God's workmanship, created in Christ Jesus to do good works, which God prepared in advance for us to do' (Ephesians 2:10).

★ ★ ★ TODAY Wednesday June 3 1992

NOSE OP MISERY REVENGE

A CHARITY worker was jailed yesterday for a vendetta against the cosmetic surgeon she believed ruined her expensive nose job.

Natasha Anderson, 27, repeatedly daubed obscenities on Anthony Erian's Harley Street surgery.

Her bizarre revenge went on for five months until police filmed her in the act.

She was remanded in custody for psychiatric reports yesterday by London's Marlborough Street magistrates after admitting six counts of criminal damage. Anderson, of Beaconsfield, Bucks, had taken four drugs overdoses since Mr Erian operated on her, the court heard.

She believed years of being tormented over her nose had ended when her father paid for cosmetic surgery. But that operation was ruined when she asked Mr Erian to improve her lips four years ago, Anderson claimed.

Before being locked up, she said: "I was very happy with my nose but he messed it all up. I wanted to die."

Smiling Natasha on her way to court yesterday

Is God interested in the way we look? Explain.

....
....
....
....
....

Is God interested in our personality and character more, less or the same as the way we look? Explain.

....
....
....
....
....

Glossy magazines emphasise physical attractiveness. What other things can make a person special?

....
....
....
....
....
....

Is everyone special, or only a few? Explain.

....
....
....
....
....

In what ways can low self-esteem affect the way a person looks, behaves talks or dresses?

....
....
....
....
....

Are good-looking people the happiest people? Explain.

....
....
....
....
....

MONEY MATTERS

MEETING AIM:
To compare what the Bible teaches about money and possessions with commonly-held materialistic values.

FOREIGN EXCHANGE (10 mins)
As the young people arrive, write a number on the back of their hand (from one to however many arrive) using a water-based felt-tip pen (this is for the gameshow later in the programme). Then hand out photocopied versions of the quizsheet below and a pen/pencil. Use this game to introduce the theme of money.

FOREIGN EXCHANGE QUIZ

Draw a line connecting the correct country with its currency:

1) Austria	a) Escudos
2) Denmark	b) Shekels
3) France	c) Livres
4) Germany	d) Drachmae
5) Greece	e) Lire
6) Holland	f) Schillings
7) Ireland	g) Rands
8) Israel	h) Guilders
9) Italy	i) Kroners
10) Portugal	j) Marks
11) South Africa	k) Francs
12) Lebanon	l) Punts

Answers: 1f, 2i, 3k, 4j, 5d, 6h, 7l, 8b, 9e, 10a, 11g, 12c.

THE PRICE IS RIGHT (20 mins)
This game, modelled on the TV gameshow, involves maximum audience participation, either as players or through wildly enthusiastic cheering/clapping.

The game begins with four people who you choose randomly by calling out numbers. If they have that number on the back of their hand, you as Master of Ceremonies (MC) invite them to 'come on down'. Encourage the rest to cheer and clap as each person is chosen.

The four contestants are then shown a picture (cut out of a catalogue) of a hi-fi, mountain bike, washing machine, etc, and asked to estimate its selling price. Describe the item using the selling blurb from the catalogue.

After the first person has had a guess at the price of the item in the catalogue, the MC then encourages the audience to help the second contestant by suggesting a higher or lower bid. They call out 'higher' or 'lower' accordingly. Have an assistant write down who bid what amount. The person who guesses closest to the price without bidding a penny more than the catalogue price is the winner of that round. That person stands aside, as they have qualified for the final stage of the contest, and a replacement is found from the audience by you calling out another number. They are told to 'come on down' from the audience (cue for more enthusiastic over-the-top applause!).

After five rounds, the first stage of the game ends. All the contestants who didn't make it to the next stage are invited to take their seats.

Now all the winners of the preliminary rounds get together to bid for further items - the only difference is that they get to keep it if they have the winning bid. This means you need to buy (and keep a record of the price) five prizes, eg pot of hair gel, large bar of chocolate, coffee mug. Encourage the audience to make appreciative 'oooh' sounds when each prize is announced. Make the final prize something a bit special that they will all want to win.

SMASH & GRAB VALUES (25 mins)
Photocopy and cut into bank note shapes the pound notes from the Royal Bank of Watford opposite. Then stuff a note into a balloon according to the formula below, and inflate and tie the balloons. Prepare at least 12 balloons for each person you expect to attend.

If possible, hang a net from the ceiling with the balloons in. An alternative is to store them in several large (fridge/freezer size) cardboard boxes. Most shops which sell electrical appliances will give you boxes this size for free if you ask. Tip them out of the boxes at the start of the game.

The object of this game is to burst all the balloons as quickly as possible and grab the fake money inside. In every 12 balloons insert two £1,000 notes, two £500, four £100, four £50.

Once all the balloons are burst and notes collected allow two minutes for everyone to count their money, then go on to the second part of the game.

Hand out bid sheets of the values auction, sponsored by the Royal Bank of Watford! Explain that they have to submit a written bid for all of the items in the auction. The smallest bid allowed is £50 and there is no upper limit so long as they have the money to pay!

Some of your group may need help with the sums required as they write down their bids, so be sure to have helpers available at this point.

Having completed all their bids, which cannot be changed in the light of what other people have bid, the young people take it in turns to shout out what they bid for item one in the auction. As they make their bid, have someone collect the necessary money from them. IOUs are not acceptable! The winning bid is the highest, but everyone's money is kept.

After each item, briefly discuss why they bid high or low. Were some people's bids surprising? Encourage those who collected only a small amount of money to talk about their frustrations at the items they wanted going to a higher bidder.

After all the items have been bid for, develop the discussion to talk about who/what influences our value systems most (parents, friends, TV adverts, etc). Ask them which values they feel they share with their parents'/grandparents' generation, and which they don't.

IN YOUR OWN WORDS (25-30 mins)
Divide the young people into small groups with a leader and ask them each to study two of the following sections of scripture: Matthew 6:31-33, Luke 18:18-25, Acts 4:32-35, Philippians 4:11-13, 1 Timothy 6:6-10.

Ask each group to study the two scripture passages and rewrite the story or advice into their own words - maximum 80 words (40 words per passage). Also ask them to make a note of anything they thought was particularly good advice and anything they disagreed with or thought was unreasonable or impractical.

Allow the groups up to 15 minutes and then get back together for feedback. Encourage them to say what they really think, rather than what they think you want them to say.

Obviously you will need to read through and study these passages yourself beforehand.

VALUE AUCTION BID SHEET
sponsored by the Royal Bank of Watford

YOUR BID

1) Top of the range mountain bike

£..

2) Football season ticket (team of your choice)

£..

3) Six hassle free months with your parent(s)

£..

4) Five minutes' free grab at favourite clothes shop

£..

5) To eliminate world hunger for a year

£..

6) A guaranteed well-paid job after school/college

£..

7) Two weeks' holiday to USA with a friend

£..

8) Top of the range computer & £250 worth of software

£..

MAKING TIME

MEETING AIM:
To help the group identify the way they use and sometimes waste their time, and to help them to prioritise their day so they use what spare time they have more effectively to reach their stated goals.

BALANCING ACT (10 mins)
For this intro game you need a long, thin beam of wood approximately 10cm x 10cm thick, plus two trays and some plastic objects.

Ask for pairs of volunteers who have a good sense of balance. Then explain that one person has to walk along the beam and back again, while holding a tray in each hand. Their partner gradually loads the trays with various objects, which should include plastic bottles filled with liquid, bean bags, etc. The person on the beam has to balance the trays and keep his or her balance on the beam. If you play this game outside, it could be done on a fallen tree with plastic cups full of water.

Either way, it should provide a good way into this weeks theme of time, and the way most people have a difficult job in balancing all their time demands.

TIME EATERS (10-15 mins)
Get the whole group to call out activities that take up a lot of time outside the nine to five of a typical job or school/college classes, eg computer games, watching TV, playing sport, shopping. Write a list up on a flipchart or onto an OHP. Ask the group to look back over the list and identify items which can eat up a lot of time if they are allowed to, eg shopping is to some extent a necessity, but beyond that it has become a leisure activity in its own right.

Then in small groups ask individuals to identify one item from the list on which they spend a lot of extra time. Allow three minutes and then get feedback. Put a tick or keep count of the main time-eater from the list which your group identifies so that you end up with a 'top three' of time-eaters for your youth group/club.

End this section by saying that part of the way in which we can reveal where our priorities lie is by identifying how we spend large parts of our leisure time. Although fishing or shopping are not wrong, where they become all-consuming activities they can limit our horizons and our ability to grow and achieve other goals (including spiritual ones).

BOGGLE (15 mins)
If you have a group which is 12 or smaller, buy, or preferably borrow from members of the church, some sets of Boggle (by MB Games). You will need one game for every four people.

If your group is bigger than 12 play a scaled-up version of the game - you will still need to buy or borrow one set of the game to get the hang of the rules.

Then by drawing variations of the 12-letter dice and boardcards onto OHPs and handing out paper and pens to everyone, you can play Boggle with a group as large as 50.

The essence of this game is that pressure and tension are created because you are playing against the clock. In fact the clock is literally a loudly ticking two-minute alarm.

Use this game to talk briefly about how so many people are pressured by time and deadlines which rule their lives.

GROUNDHOG DAY (10 mins)
Rent and watch this video which stars Bill Murray. Select a clip from the early part of the film (which most of your group are likely to have seen) which shows the main character going through the routine of his day. Put the clip in context and explain the main plot of the film - that this man is locked into one day which he relives over and over again. Eventually he learns to treat the people he meets during his day better.

Make the point that we do not have the opportunity to live any part of our lives (a day, an hour or even a minute) over again, although often we might wish we could so that we could put something right or change the way we said or did something.

But now, instead of looking into the past, let's look into the future of time.

(NB: I am not recommending that you show your group the whole film, which may contain unsuitable scenes.)

GROUNDHOG YEAR (10-15 mins)
In small groups, ask people to share their answer to the question:

'Imagine that you learned that you would die in exactly one year from today. How would you use that time differently from the way you currently expect to spend the year?'

Allow five to 10 minutes in small groups, then encourage feedback.

Be sensitive to any members of the group who may have family or friends who are seriously ill, or if they are grieving a recent death of someone close to them.

TOO BUSY? (10 mins)
Divide the group into two and allocate one half to take on the role of Mary and the other Martha in the story you are about to read out. Ask everyone to really try to get into the character.

Suggest everyone closes their eyes, then slowly read out Luke 10:38-42 (you may want to read it through twice). Then ask people to talk about how they felt.

Mary (peaceful, pleased to be spending time with Jesus).

Martha (rushed, resentful that Mary wasn't helping, humbled by what Jesus said).

SAY: 'Mary's priority in that story was to spend time with Jesus. Martha's priority was to prepare a meal for Jesus. Whether you tend to be more like Mary or Martha, the fact is we all make priorities of how we use our time, whether we realise it or not.

One useful way to prioritise our time is to set goals we want to achieve.'

GOAL SETTING (10 mins)
Hand out pens and photocopies of the sheet opposite, and ask everyone to identify which of the goals they think are clear goals, and which they think are fuzzy (unclear) goals. Allow two minutes, then give the answers: (The odd-numbered goals are fuzzy, the even numbers are clear.)

Then make the point that for a goal to be clear it needs to be specific and measurable.

SAY: 'The first goal on the sheet is fuzzy because it isn't measurable or specific - there is no time frame with which to measure yourself. Besides, what is the definition of 'fit'?

'By comparison, goal number two is both clear and measurable. By Christmas you will know whether you have achieved that goal.'

Having made that point, ask everyone to complete their own goal statement at the bottom of the sheet. The goal should relate to use of time, but can be linked to anything - spiritual, physical, to do with exams, friendships and so on. However, encourage them to make the goal specific and measurable.

TIME FOR EVERYTHING (2 mins)
Read out Ecclesiastes 3:1-8 which says there is time for everything. Then close the meeting by praying that everyone will spend their time (days, year, life) wisely and well.

CLEAR TARGET?

Which of the following statements are clear aims and which are fuzzy? Put an ↗ in the centre of each target for clear or in the tinted area for fuzzy.

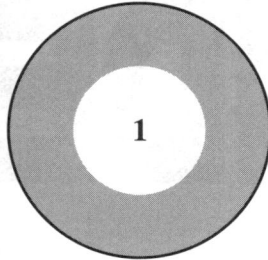

1) I want to get fit as soon as possible.

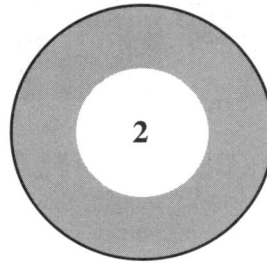

2) I want to become a qualified First Aid-er by Christmas.

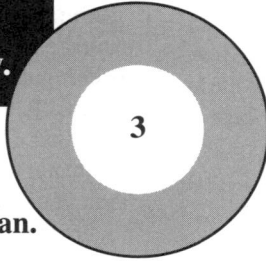

3) I want to become a better Christian.

4) I want to read a chapter from the Bible every day for a month.

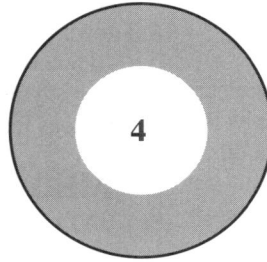

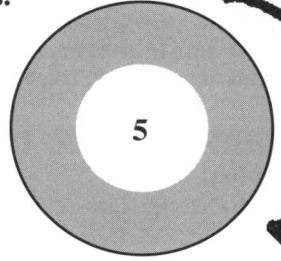

5) I want to learn to drive.

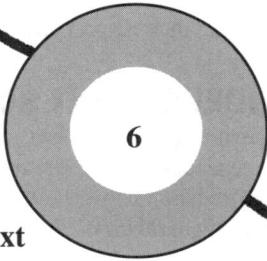

6) I want to watch every episode of Neighbours during the next school holiday.

7) I want to be kinder to my youth leader.

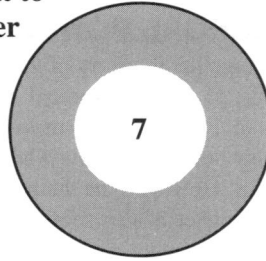

8) I want to achieve two or more grade 'A's in my next school report.

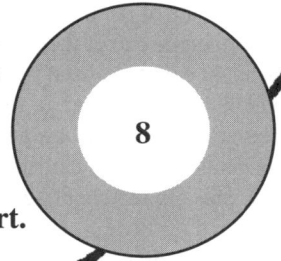

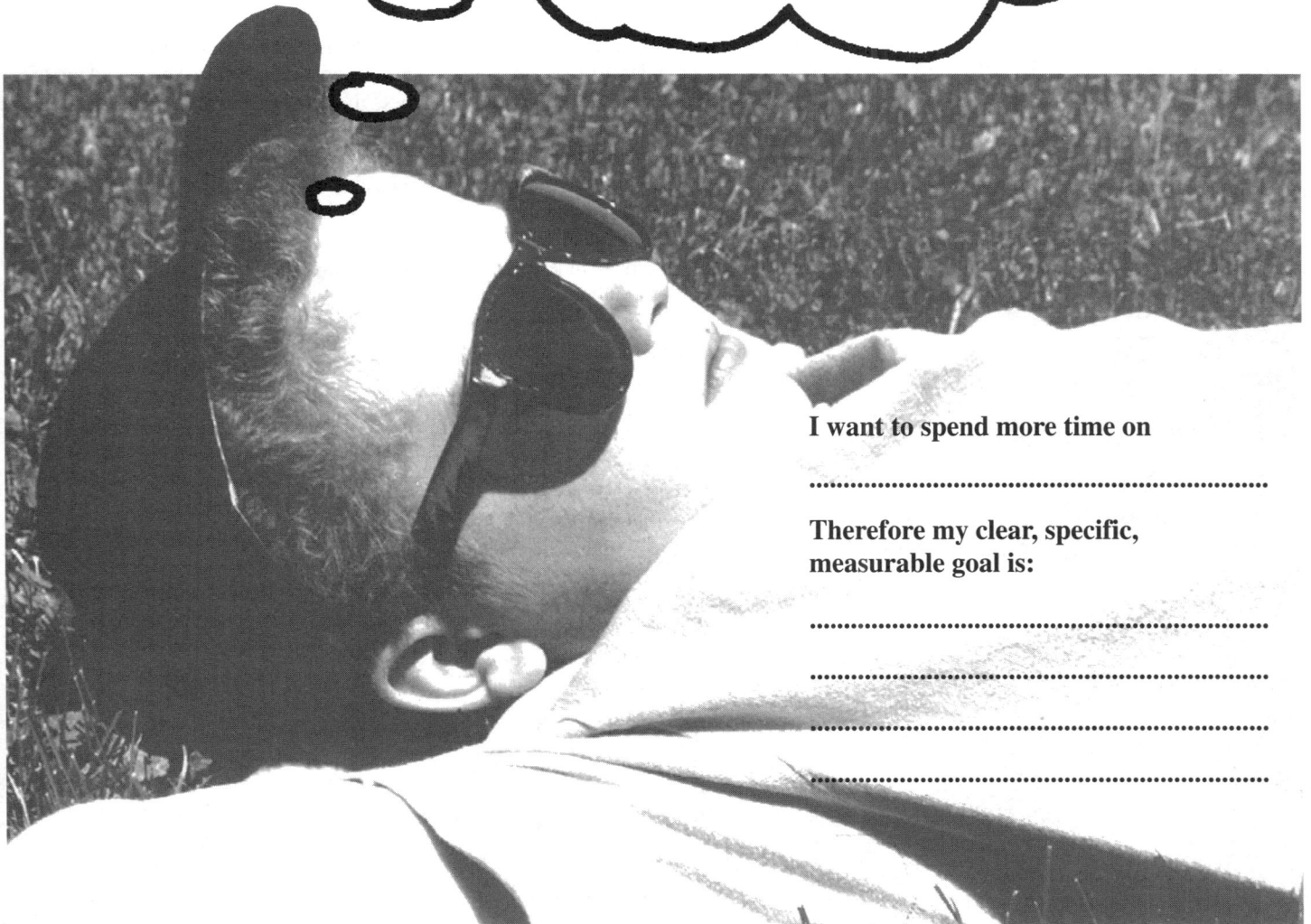

I want to spend more time on

....

Therefore my clear, specific, measurable goal is:

....

....

....

....

INDEPENDENCE

MEETING AIM:
To help young people discover what the Bible says about gaining independence, and explore ways to avoid arguments with parents about gaining independence.

INDEPENDENCE INTRO (5 mins)
On 9th October Uganda annually celebrates its independence from former rule by Britain.

Explain to your youth group that this week's theme is independence - how it is gained and the responsibilities it brings.

Focus on one country, eg Uganda or another which has its independence date on or near the date of the meeting (eg, Kenya - 12 December, or one of the newly independent countries from the former Soviet Union). You could go the whole hog by decorating the room with posters from travel agents and/or the embassy of the country, plus the national flag, stamps and so on.

Compare the difficulties some countries faced gaining independence (coping with new-found freedom) with the stresses that affect young people as they become more independent of their parents.

DESIGN A FLAG (10 mins)
SAY: 'Imagine that your city/town/village has become independent of the rest of the UK. Design a flag for your newly independent country. The design should somehow symbolise or represent what the town is like, or what you want it to be like!'

Photocopy the flag worksheet opposite and provide felt-tip pens, etc. Compare flags and reasons for designs.

KING FOR A DAY (5 mins)
SAY: 'If you were the ruler of this newly independent country, what three new rules or laws would you introduce and why?'

PRODIGAL POWER (15 mins)
Read together the story of the Prodigal Son in Luke 15:11-32 ('prodigal' means *wasteful, reckless*). Jesus told this parable to show how glad God is when we repent of our sins. However, the theme of independence is also strong in this story about the younger son who cheekily asks for his inheritance before his father dies. As he was unmarried it is most likely that the younger son was no older than 19. Leaving home with plenty of money gave him independence, but he wasn't mature enough to cope with this sudden total freedom.

Ask the following questions:
● Why did the younger son make such a mess of his new-found independence? (He was immature. It was sudden independence instead of gradual. He wasn't used to handling money.)
● How can being reckless with the freedom our parents give us destroy or damage our relationship with our parents? (They lose their trust in us. It could affect the way we talk/communicate.)
● What is the best way to win more independence from our parents? (Show we can be responsible with the limited freedom they currently allow us, calmly and lovingly asking for an extension of the freedom they allow us within reasonable limits, accepting their decision without losing our temper if they say 'no', and then asking again some weeks later.)

SAY: 'Becoming more independent is a natural part of growing into an adult. Your parents/guardians may sometimes be strict, but usually this is, in their opinion, for your own good. Going to war with your parents in an attempt to win more independence will harm your relationship with them and may not get you what you want either. A better response is to learn from your past mistakes and earn their respect and trust.'

INDEPENDENT SOAP (10 mins)
The most popular Aussie soaps on our TV screens regularly feature rows and confrontation between children and parents/guardians over issues relating to independence (eg staying out late, choice of friends).

Video and then show a short clip from an episode to spark a discussion on what restrictions to their independence your group's own parent(s) make, and which of these they consider unreasonable.

ASK: 'If you were totally independent of your parents/guardians, what would you choose to do that is currently forbidden or restricted?'

DIGGING DEEPER (15 mins)
Read Galatians 5:1, then ask:
● What does God think about being free?
● What sort of freedom is this verse about?
Read Galatians 5:13, then ask:
● What is one of the biggest dangers of independence and freedom according to this verse?
Read Ephesians 6:1-3, then ask:
● What do you do which most annoys your parents?
● What do you think it means to 'honour' your parents?

DECLARATION OF INDEPENDENCE (10 mins)
In groups of two or three write down some specific things parents could do to give their children more independence. Share the ideas and encourage the young people to take the list home to talk through some of the issues. However, encourage them to see things from their parents'/guardians' viewpoint as well.

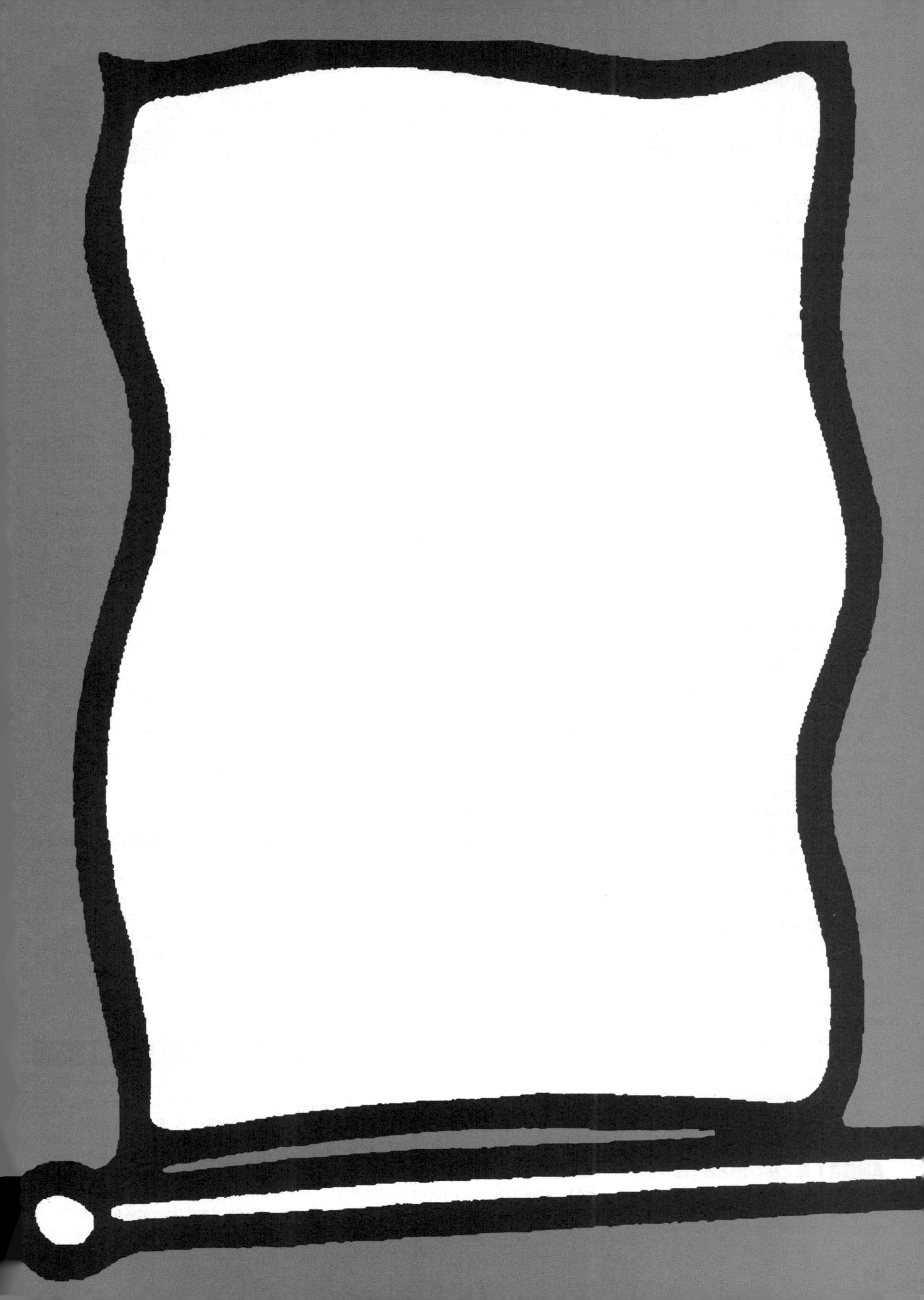

AGGRO

MEETING AIM:
To identify the destructive power of uncontrolled anger and to teach that God also gets angry and that this has implications.

LOSE YOUR COOL (5 mins)

Prearrange the following with a suitable member of your group. It will certainly start your meeting with a surprise.

Begin by reading out a list of non-important notices. During this time the person begins to interrupt and heckle you. Respond by politely asking him or her to be quiet and listen. The person continues to interrupt and make smart alec comments. (This will need a rehearsal to make it convincing!)

After about five minutes of this suddenly blow up, order the person out, and shout after them that you never want to see them again.

Allow a silent pause. While everyone, including helpers who were not in on this, look at each other in shock. Then calmly read: 'People with a hot temper do foolish things; wiser people remain calm. If you stay calm, you are wise, but if you have a hot temper, you only show how stupid you are' (Proverbs 14:17,29, GNB).

Explain that the theme of this week's meeting is anger. Then invite the person who you shouted at, to join the group again. Encourage a round of applause for their Oscar-winning performance.

SAY: 'When a person gets angry, it can be quite disturbing and shocking. Anger can be a very destructive emotion. But is it always wrong to get angry?'

MR ANGRY (10 mins)

Show a clip from the film *Clockwise* which stars John Cleese as a punctual headmaster. Select a clip where Cleese loses his temper. Probably the best scene for this is where the car gets stuck in the mud and he tries to push it out - and fails! If you can't get hold of this film from your video shop, use an alternative short clip from a film which has a scene where someone loses their temper and gets mad. There are lots of films to choose from!

ANGRY MEMORIES (15 mins)

Write the list *(right)* onto an OHP screen or whiteboard and get people to share their responses in small groups. Allow up to 10 minutes in small groups and then get the

LETTING OFF STEAM (10 mins)

Play a contact game such as uni-hock, five-a-side or basketball. This will have the effect of giving people's brains a few minutes to relax, plus opportunities for them to start to put into practice what they are learning about dealing with anger!

groups together for feedback.

I get angry when...

Once I lost my temper because...

I am glad I got angry/lost my temper because...

I regret getting angry/losing my temper because...

ANGER ADVICE (10 mins)

SAY: 'Anger is a powerful emotion and it can affect our ability to make sensible and wise decisions.

'Anger can lead to violence, which can vary from slamming a door to smashing a plate; from hitting someone with your fist to stabbing a person to death. Uncontrolled anger is a frightening and destructive emotion.

'So what does the Bible say about how a Christian should deal with anger?'

Read Proverbs 15:1, 18 and Ephesians 4:25-5:2, then ask:

- What advice do these passages give?
- What practical advice do you have which helps you control your temper?

AN ANGRY GOD (10-15 mins)

SAY: 'Anger can take a positive form, when the anger is used for good. It results in an attempt to correct the situation - not just react in a violent way to the wrong-doer. This positive anger can be used on your own behalf or for other people. Many campaigns to put right an injustice have started from this type of anger.

'God gets angry sometimes too - but when he does it is justified and always in control.'

Read Amos 8:4-7, then in small groups or all together ask:

- Who was God angry with and why?
- What other examples of God or Jesus getting angry are recorded in the Bible?
- What individuals / groups / companies / nations do you think God is angry with today and why?
- How can a loving and caring God get angry?

CONFLICT DILEMMAS (15 mins)

Hand out copies of the worksheet opposite and allow up to 10 minutes for them to be completed. You may need to give some background information on the four characters featured (Martin Luther King, Robin Hood, Gandhi and Mother Teresa).

During a coffee break get people to feed back their answers/responses and let that spark off discussion and debate.

OPTIONAL EXTRA

Show part or all of the feature-length film *The Hiding Place*. This tells the story of Corrie ten Boom and her family who sheltered Jews from the invading Germans in Holland during World War Two. Despite being sent to a concentration camp with her sister, who died there, Corrie learned how to deal with anger and bitterness towards the German camp guards, and she came to forgive them.

IF AT SCHOOL, SOMEONE STARTS TO PICK ON YOU BECAUSE OF YOUR LOOKS WHAT WOULD YOU DO?

WHAT IS THE BEST WAY, IN YOUR OPINION, TO HELP THE POOR?

WHAT WAY DOES GOD SAY WE SHOULD SOLVE OUR PROBLEMS?

DOES GOD EVER SAY VIOLENCE IS OK?

SEX

MEETING AIM:

To introduce the subject of sex and to help you to assess what other, more detailed, teaching and advice on relationships and sex you need to supply. This outline covers three stages: looking at the assumptions of today's society; exploring what the Christian viewpoint is supposed to be; then probing where your young people find it most difficult to follow Jesus' ideal.

MEETING PREPARATION

Survey a group of 10 people (eg parents, older people in the church, or young people who do not belong to your group/club), asking them to agree or disagree with the following six statements:

● **It's very difficult for teenage boys not to be obsessed by pornography.**

● **Staying a virgin is not easy for most 15-year-olds.**

● **It's curiosity, not lust or love, that usually leads teenagers into sexual activity.**

● **AIDS doesn't really worry teenagers.**

● **Masturbation is sinful and young people should be told that clearly.**

● **Many young Christians can't see why practising homosexuality is wrong.**

Keep the scores, you will need them.

To start people thinking and talking about the subject straight away, it might be good to prepare the room before the start of the evening by scattering around some postcards bearing quotes about sex made by famous people. (Almost any mass circulation magazine will provide a selection!)

BRAINWASHED (10 mins)

Separate the group into two teams. Explain to Team A that they must question the other side about the first time they were kissed. But the question mustn't be asked directly: instead, Team A must ask questions like: 'How long did it take?', 'Was anyone else there?', 'Did you enjoy it?', 'Were you glad you'd done it afterwards?', and so on. In exchange, they have to answer Team B's questions - which will be about how Team A used to spend playtime when in infant school.

Explain to Team B that they are going to be asked some questions about how they spent last Saturday afternoon. They must not name the activity they were engaged in, but can answer questions about it which will not give the game away. In return they can ask Team A questions about the first romantic relationship they ever had with a member of the opposite sex. Team B must not ask about it directly, but ask questions like: 'How old were you at the time?', 'How long did it last?', 'Did you do this with more than one person at the same time?'

Then let them talk to one another - and watch the confusion. Often people realise quite soon that something is wrong, but the results are so hilarious that they keep going anyway. Call a halt before it runs out of steam, and say: 'The trouble with that conversation was that neither side really knew what was going on. Because they had a distorted view of the situation, they kept giving the wrong responses. They had a wrong picture in their minds.

'The same is true when you look at what people make of sex in our society. They have been brainwashed by media and popular opinion into taking a distorted view and responding to sex in a way God never intended. Their picture is all wrong'.

IN THE NEWS (10 mins)

Divide the young people into groups, asking them to write down the names of people in the news who:
(a) are having an affair with someone they're not married to;
(b) have used their body in a non-Christian way to achieve success;
(c) have said things about sex which the Bible wouldn't agree with;
(d) live a practising homosexual or bisexual lifestyle;
(e) have been through several sexual partners.

WHAT DOES GOD SAY?
(5 mins)

Read Romans 12:1-2 (GNB).
Make the point that this world has 'standards' to which it wants us to 'conform ourselves'. But being a Christian means that we 'offer' ourselves as 'a living sacrifice to God' and put our body at his disposal. If we do this we will 'be able to know the will of God'; if not, we will simply end up confused and compromised.

J.B. Phillips translated verse 2: 'Don't let the world squeeze you into its mould.' Let's look at some of the materials that are trying to mould us.

AGONY AUNT/UNCLE
(15-20 mins)

Get your youngsters into same sex groups of two's or three's and give each group a photocopy of the appropriate half of the page opposite (agony aunt letter for girls, agony uncle letter for lads). Each group should compose a letter with three pieces of advice which could include a biblical perspective.

Share the results after revealing that Debbie and Dave are going out with each other. Ask for opinions of the quality of the advice given, and then sit back as the discussion hots up!

N.B. The quality of this activity will partly depend on how well you have prepared. It could just be a way for people to share their ignorance – or it could be a springboard towards checking out what scripture says. Have a number of Bible references ready to feed into the discussion if needed.

OPINION GUESS (10 mins)

Now read out the statements on which you collected opinions before the meeting. Tell them who you surveyed, and let the group guess what the results were. Their responses here are very important; they will yield a lot of insight into what they really think, what their opinions are, and - most important - which issues are genuine problems for them which you need to address in subsequent programmes. Then tell them how your respondents actually did vote, and, again, watch how they react.

CONCLUSION (10 mins)

Read Proverbs 5:15-22. Split into small groups to discuss:
1. How important does the Bible think sex is?
2. Can you find at least three reasons here for keeping sex inside marriage? Do they make sense?
3. Can you find at least three reasons here for avoiding casual sex? Do they make sense?

Sum up the main lessons you've learned, and end by making it clear that you're available to talk to anyone who wants to discuss this further.

End in prayer and leave a time of silence when people can quietly and privately offer up three things to God: the questions they still don't understand, any mistakes they've made, and any promises they want to make to him.

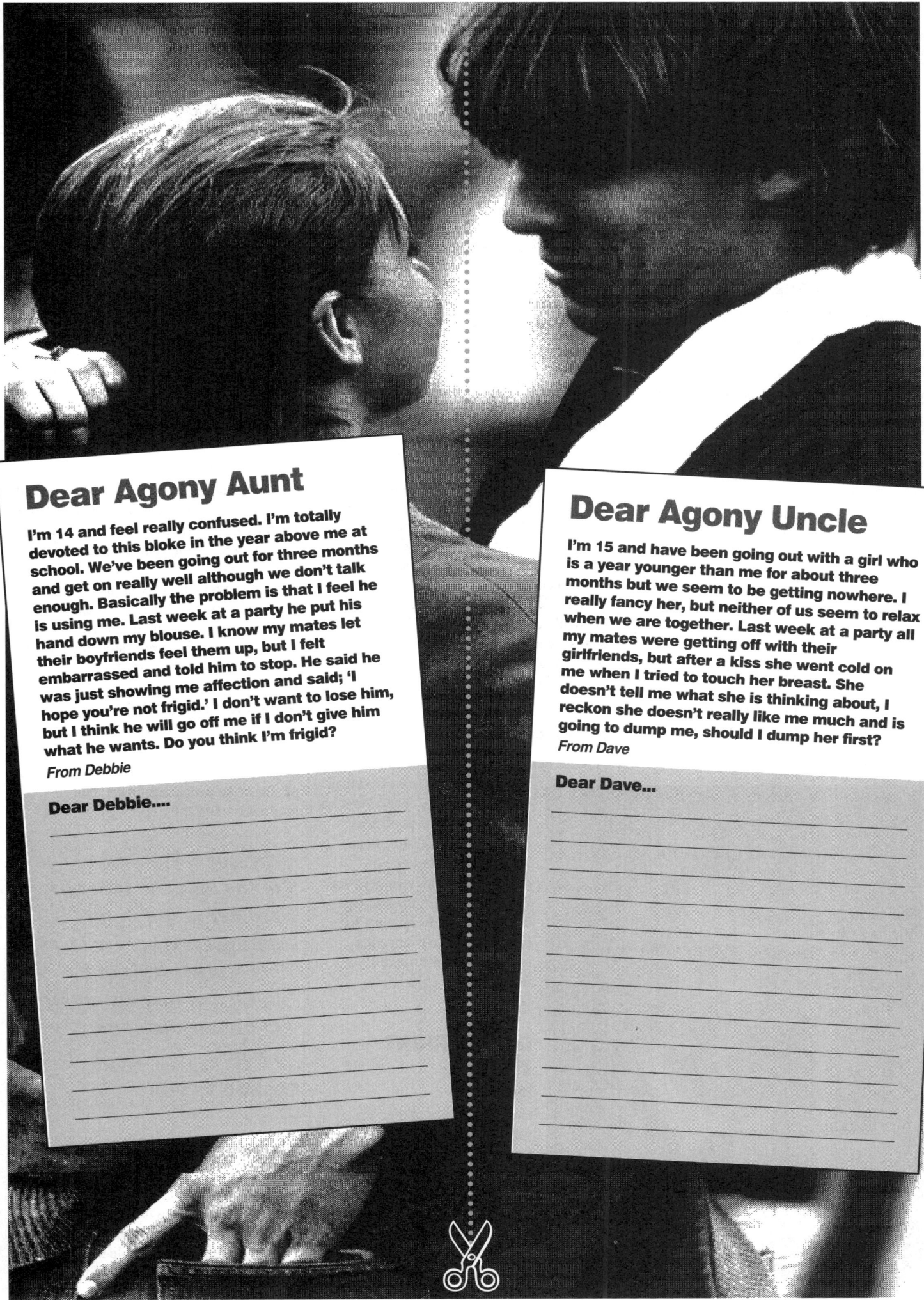

Dear Agony Aunt

I'm 14 and feel really confused. I'm totally devoted to this bloke in the year above me at school. We've been going out for three months and get on really well although we don't talk enough. Basically the problem is that I feel he is using me. Last week at a party he put his hand down my blouse. I know my mates let their boyfriends feel them up, but I felt embarrassed and told him to stop. He said he was just showing me affection and said; 'I hope you're not frigid.' I don't want to lose him, but I think he will go off me if I don't give him what he wants. Do you think I'm frigid?

From Debbie

Dear Debbie....

_____
_____
_____
_____
_____
_____
_____
_____
_____
_____
_____

Dear Agony Uncle

I'm 15 and have been going out with a girl who is a year younger than me for about three months but we seem to be getting nowhere. I really fancy her, but neither of us seem to relax when we are together. Last week at a party all my mates were getting off with their girlfriends, but after a kiss she went cold on me when I tried to touch her breast. She doesn't tell me what she is thinking about, I reckon she doesn't really like me much and is going to dump me, should I dump her first?

From Dave

Dear Dave...

_____
_____
_____
_____
_____
_____
_____
_____
_____
_____
_____

HONESTY

MEETING AIM:
To emphasise the value and importance that God places on honesty, and to underline that lies often affect more people than just the liar.

THE BIG PORK PIE (10 mins)

Viewers of BBC TV's Noel Edmonds' House Party will know how this game works. Ideally you should watch this programme before trying this game. An unsuspecting member of the audience is identified and invited to take part in this game. He or she has been 'set up' by a friend or family member. The audience are then let in on the secret from the person's past, for example they might have had an operation to change the shape of their nose, but told people they had fallen off a moving train.

The 'volunteer' is then asked a series of questions. They are encouraged to lie convincingly. After four or five questions comes the big fib. Award a large pork pie to the participant.

Sum up by saying that some people are better at lying than others, but all of us have had some practice from time to time!

It goes without saying that you need to choose the person to take part in this game with care. It may be best to select an adult

Noel Edmonds

volunteer helper, but here too avoid using someone who might not be able to take this as a joke.

20 FIBS (10 mins)

Play this fibbing variation of the game 20 Questions. All the young people play together as one team and have to guess the identity of a person by asking up to 20 questions. The person can be living or dead, or even a fictional character from a book, play or film. To avoid chaos, one of the young people is nominated as the questioner, and he or she acts as the spokesperson for the group.

The twist to this game is that the answers the young people are given are all lies. For example, if the identity of the person was Bill Clinton and the question came, 'Is this person male?' the answer would be 'no'.

This requires lots of extra concentration from all concerned.

Conclude by saying: 'Telling lies makes life really complicated and difficult. But the fact is we all tell lies from time to time. Why? And are lies ever OK, even the right thing to do in certain situations? Let's investigate.'

SAMUEL'S STORY (5 mins)

Tell the story of the boy Samuel who was given a message from God that Eli the priest (his master) and his family were to be punished because of their disobedience (1 Samuel 3). Underline how difficult it would have been for Samuel to tell Eli the message honestly and how he must have been tempted to change the message to make it more favourable, or even tell an outright lie.

DO THE RIGHT THING
(20 mins)

Hand out copies of the worksheet opposite. Having read through the story and decided what their response would be, get feedback and encourage some discussion on the rights and wrongs of the story.

Next get the young people to complete the second assignment. Allow five minutes, then go

round the group and ask them to read out their rewrite of Psalm 15.

THE BEST POLICY? (10 mins)

Write the following statements onto an acetate and project it on an OHP. Ask the young people to give each statement a score from one (completely disagree) to 10 (completely agree).

● **Lying is OK... if you don't get caught.**

● **Honesty is the best policy.**

● **A little white lie doesn't do much harm.**

● **Lies breed more lies.**

Then tell a true story of how a lie you told got you into trouble, or how someone else's lie got you into trouble. Ask whether any of the young people have had similar experiences.

Aim to sum up by making the point that lies can be very destructive. Often we are tempted to lie to get out of a tricky situation, but it can result in more trouble than if we had told the truth at the start.

THE GOOD NEWS (3 mins)

Read out 1 John 1:9-10 and underline that if we are truly sorry God forgives us from lies as well as all other sins. Allow for a moment of silence so people can make their confessions to God.

> *Anyone who claims to be in the light but hates his brother is still in the darkness. Whoever loves his brother lives in the light, and there is nothing in him to make him stumble.*
>
> **1 John 1 v 9-10**

AN HONEST MAN (3 mins)

End by reading out or telling the story from 1 Samuel 12:1-5. At the end of his life the people Samuel judged told him he had been fair and honest with everyone.

Challenge the young people to ask themselves whether others would say the same about them.

A thief's lucky day

Victim hands back highway robber's £25,000 lottery ticket

A THIEF who dropped a winning lottery ticket at the scene of his crime has been given a lesson in honesty.

His victim, who picked up the ticket, then claimed the £25,000 prize, managed to trace him and handed over the cash.

The robbery happened when maths professor Vincio Sabbatucci, 58, was changing a tyre on an Italian motorway.

Another motorist, who stopped 'to help', stole a suitcase from his car and drove off.

The professor found the dropped ticket and stuffed it into his pocket before driving home to Ascoli in eastern Italy.

Next day, he saw the lottery results on TV and, uncrumpling the ticket, realised it was a winner. He claimed the £25,000 prize.

Reported by Ronald Singleton from the Daily Mail 17 January 1994.

Then began a battle with his conscience. Eventually he decided that he could not keep the money despite having been robbed.

He advertised in newspapers and on radio, saying: 'I'm trying to find the man who robbed me. I have £25,000 for him - a lottery win. Please meet me. Anonymity guaranteed.'

Professor Sabbatucci received hundreds of calls from people hoping to trick him into handing them the cash.

But there was one voice he recognised - and he arranged to meet the man in a park.

The robber, a 35-year-old unemployed father of two, gave back the suitcase and burst into tears.

He could not believe what was happening. 'Why didn't you keep the money?' he asked.

The professor replied: 'I couldn't because it's not mine.'

Then he walked off, spurning the thief's offer of a reward.

What would you have done? *(tick one box)*

☐ Keep the money and keep quiet.

☐ Contact the police, explain about the robbery and the lottery ticket win, give them the prize money and let the legal system take over.

☐ Give the prize money to charity.

☐ Contact the robber like the professor and hand him the money.

☐ Other ....
....
....

Rewrite Psalm 15 below in your own words
(maximum 40).

Lord, who may enter your Holy Tent? Who may live on your holy mountain? Only those who are innocent and who do what is right. Such people speak the truth from their hearts and do not tell lies about others. They do no wrong to their neighbours and do not gossip. They do not respect hateful people but honour those who honour the Lord. They keep their promises to their neighbours, even when it hurts. They do not charge interest on money they lend and do not take money to hurt innocent people.

Whoever does all these things will never be destroyed.

Scripture quoted from The Youth Bible, New Century Version (Anglicised Edition) © 1993 by Nelson Word Ltd, 9 Holdom Ave, Bletchley, Milton Keynes MK1 1QR.

LIVING A LIE

MEETING AIM:
To challenge the group to practise what they preach and avoid criticising others for hypocrisy, while also seeing that if they are living a lie, they can ask God's forgiveness and start again.

DOUBLE WORDS (12-15 mins)
Hand out a pen and a copy of the Double Words quiz sheet to each person. Give a suitable prize (Double Mint chewing gum, or a Double Decker chocolate bar) to the person who completes the sheet first or who has most correct answers.

ANSWERS: 1) Bed 2) Glazed 3) Chin 4) Bass 5) Decker 6) Barrelled 7) Cream 8) Cross 9) Edged 10) Dutch 11) Quick 12) Jointed 13) Time 14) Check 15) Dealing 16) Breasted 17) Entendre 18) Take

EXPERT FIBS (15 mins)
Arrange two chairs in front of the rest of the group and sit in one. Announce that you are the host of a brand new TV chat show and that tonight you have some really interesting guests.

Then invite the first of the volunteers to join you (prearrange this by asking for up to three volunteers, but give little info on what they need to do).

Introduce the 'guest' with something like: 'Ladies and gentlemen, please welcome Lord Dibble of Devonshire, a foremost expert in antiques.'

Proceed to ask several questions of the guest about their area of expertise. They should try to appear knowledgeable about the subject. Ask questions which cannot be answered by one word answers.

Keep the interview fairly short (3 mins) unless the 'expert' is really doing well.

Conclude this game by explaining that the theme for this week is hypocrisy. Then read out the following dictionary definition of hypocrisy:

Hypocrisy - from Greek *hypokrisia*, acting or playing a part, pretending to be better than one is, or to be what one is not; concealment of true character or belief.

THEN SAY: 'Of all human failings and sin hypocrisy is one which almost everyone really dislikes when they spot it in someone else. But the fact is that most people at some time in their lives have been some sort of hypocrite - pretending they are someone or that they believe in something, when it isn't true.'

HYPOCRITES IN THE NEWS (10 mins)
Collect stories from recent newspapers of people who were exposed as hypocrites, and get the young people to comment on the stories. In the unlikely event of you being unable to find any examples, refer to singer Chris de Burgh who wrote his best-selling song 'Lady in Red' in honour of his wife Dianne. But in June 1994 Chris was exposed as having had an affair with the family's teenage nanny after Dianne nearly died in a freak riding accident. He even referred to the nanny in a song '*Blond Hair, Blue Jeans*', which includes a description of how he wants to 'get her in my life, any way at all'.

Point out that it is not only politicians or TV personalities who are guilty of double standards and hypocrisy, but that they tend to be the ones who get the attention of tabloid newspapers.

Christians and the church are often criticised as being hypocritical. Ask the group to identify what specific criticisms of double standards are levelled at Christians and the church. Are these fair?

BIBLICAL HYPOCRITES (25 mins)
In small groups of up to four, ask the young people to study the following Bible passages which look at one specific hypocrite and one group of hypocrites. Ask the young people to explain why God had such a good relationship with David after what he had done, and by comparison why Jesus was so hard on the Pharisees, who at first glance were not so bad as David.

STUDY:
David: 2 Samuel 11-12:25; Psalm 51; Acts 13:22
Pharisees: Matthew 6:1-6; 7:1-5; 15:1-9; 23:13-32

STUDY BACKGROUND:
The Pharisees, the religious leaders wanted people to see them as 'holy' so they prayed in public and rigidly obeyed the letter of the Law from the Old Testament. Minor things such as diet, and other religious observances, got plenty of attention. Jesus saw right through their public self-righteousness and taught that although there is a place for public prayer, private communication with God is at the heart of a living relationship with God.

Jesus also criticised the over-critical judgement of the Pharisees. He didn't excuse wrong-doing but called for people to be discerning rather than negative, and to remember that God is the final Judge.

Matthew 23:24 sums up Jesus' reaction. The Pharisees strained their water so they didn't swallow a gnat (an unclean insect according to the Law) - they were meticulous about the details of ceremonial cleanliness, but they had lost sight of the importance of inner purity and holiness. Although ceremonially clean on the outside, they had wicked hearts.

David committed several sins in the episode with Bathsheba: he abandoned his troops by deciding not to join them (2 Samuel 11:1); he gave in to temptation (11:4); he tried to cover up his sin by deceit (11:6f); he committed murder (11:15).

But when his sin was exposed he repented (12:13). He wrote Psalm 51 at this time. David was sincere in his repentance. When we truly repent God forgives, although sin will still have a consequence. David also wrote Psalm 32 to express his happiness after he received God's forgiveness.

Explain that God loved David because although he made some terrible mistakes during his life, he was quick to confess his sins. His confessions were genuine and he didn't take God's forgiveness lightly or for granted.

CREDIBILITY GAP (5 mins)
Close the meeting by outlining that everyone goes through a time in their life when what they say (beliefs) might not tie up with what they do (actions). This credibility gap is what we call hypocrisy. But the funny thing is that while we can see hypocrisy in other people's lives, we find it hard to see and then deal with it in ourselves.

Jesus talked about people who criticised a minor failure in other people but couldn't spot the major failing in their own life (splinters and planks in the eye). We shouldn't be quick to criticise other people's failings, but instead we should keep an eye on our own behaviour and standards.

We need to practise what we preach - especially if we are a Christian - otherwise we might put people off Jesus rather than be an attractive advert for the faith.

End by emphasising that while we might be able to deceive other people, we can't pull the wool over God's eyes.

DOUBLE WORDS

All the blanks below can be filled with a word which follows 'double'. Read the clues and see how many double words you can identify. (see the example below)

1) **DOUBLE** BED — Sleeping place for two people

2) **DOUBLE** .... Two pieces of glass

3) **DOUBLE** .... Fleshy fold on the face

4) **DOUBLE** .... Largest instrument in the violin family

5) **DOUBLE** .... Two-levelled bus

6) **DOUBLE** .... Firearm or surname with two parts

7) **DOUBLE** .... 48% butterfat, suitable for whipping

8) **DOUBLE** .... An act of betrayal

9) **DOUBLE** .... Having two possible interpretations

10) **DOUBLE** .... Gibberish

11) **DOUBLE** .... Very fast

12) **DOUBLE** .... Exceptionally flexible part of the body

13) **DOUBLE** .... Payment of a worker at twice the regular wage

14) **DOUBLE** .... Take two looks

15) **DOUBLE** .... Underhand or deceitful action

16) **DOUBLE** .... Front fastening with one half of the front overlapping the other

17) **DOUBLE** .... Doubtful word, one of whose meanings is dubious

18) **DOUBLE** .... Delayed reaction to a surprising situation

GOING GREEN

MEETING AIM:
To raise awareness that God requires us to be good caretakers of his world.

DESIGNER LABEL
Enlarge and photocopy onto an acetate or onto A3 or A2 format paper the designer label image below. Use it as a logo for the theme of this week's meeting. You could also use it as the centre-piece of an invite card or poster to attract new members.

— Designer Label

LITTER PATROL (25 mins)
Put people into pairs and hand each twosome a plastic bin bag. Then go to your nearest park or open space and spend 15 minutes collecting litter. Dispose of your litter-full bin bags thoughtfully, then report back to your meeting venue, where everyone should clean their hands thoroughly. (You may want to issue gardening/plastic gloves for this exercise.)

Then ask everyone:
● What were the commonest items of litter found?
● What does 'away' mean when you throw something away?
● How can we best encourage people to take better care of the environment? (Education, higher fines, etc.)
● Have so-called 'green' issues anything to do with the Christian faith? Is God interested in whether we recycle paper or glass?

VIDEO VIEW (5 mins)
Show the CTVC video The Lord is my Shepherd. Against the background of the 23rd Psalm, powerful and disturbing images of pain, suffering and pollution of people, animals and the environment eloquently contrast.

Lasting only five minutes, this video is an excellent visual introduction to the rest of the meeting. It is available from good Christian bookshops for sale (£14.95) or hire, or from CTVC Video, Hillside Studios, Merry Hill Road, Bushey, Herts WD2 1DR. Tel: 081-950 4426.

ECO TIME-BOMB (20-25 mins)
Hand out copies of the eco time-bomb worksheet and a pen/pencil to everyone in your group. Ask them to work on their own to prioritise from the list of 14 ecological problems which they think is the most important problem, then second most important and so on.

Point out that a brief explanation of each problem is given at the bottom of the worksheet.

Allow four minutes for this exercise. Then get the young people to form small groups of between three and five members. The group compares answers and then has to formulate a group choice of priorities. Encourage groups to reach a consensus decision through discussion and debate. Explain that you expect this may take some time and allow at least 15 minutes, but you may need to give the groups longer.

Then ask each group to read out its list and explain the reasoning behind its decisions, plus details of the items it had most difficulty deciding on.

GREEN TALK (15 mins)
Read Genesis 1:25-28; 2:8-9 and Joel 2:21-27, then ask:
● From these readings, do you think God wants us to strip the earth of its resources or take good care of the world?
● What examples are there of humankind harnessing and using the world in a non-polluting and non-exploitative way?
● Does the Bible teach that humankind are equal to animals or rules over them?

Explain that an increasing number of people get their ideas about creation and ecology from the New Age movement. New Agers borrow a lot of ideas from Eastern religions and philosophies that teach we are equal in status with animals, insects, even plants and rocks. They see everything as equal and believe that both humans, animals, plants and minerals are divine. This belief which regards God as in everything is called 'pantheism'.

Although the Bible teaches that we should respect and not abuse creation, it also teaches that people are uniquely different from the rest of God's creation because we are made in God's image (Genesis 1:26).

God has trusted us with the care of his world but he remains closely interested. The Bible teaches that God knows and is interested in the smallest detail of life on planet earth.

Read Romans 8:18-25. Sin has affected creation as well as human beings, and Paul teaches that all creation looks forward to a day when it will be made whole again.

Some Christians treat this as a good excuse to be careless about looking after the world, while others believe that we are responsible for being part of the healing process.

GREEN RESOURCES

50 Ways You Can Help Save the Planet by Tony Campolo and Gordon Aeschilman (Kingsway) provides 50 down-to-earth practical suggestions for doing something about the environment in which we all live.

Whose Earth? This video will stir up interest in local and international environmental action. Available from: Tear Fund, 100 Church Road, Teddington, Middlesex TW11 8QE.

How Green Is Your Church? This pack and video includes an environmental 'audit' on your church. Available from: Christian Ecology Link, 11 Greenbank Gardens, Fareham, Hants PO16 8SF.

Creation Care Eight-page, full-colour booklet crammed with info and ideas. Available from: Evangelical Alliance, 186 Kennington Park Road, London SE11 4BT (£1.50 inc p & p).

Approved Product Guide Lists cosmetics, toiletries and household products which are not tested on animals. Available from: BUAV, 16a Crane Road, London N7 8LB.

ECO-TIME BOMB

LOOK THROUGH THE LIST BELOW THEN DECIDE WHICH IS THE MOST PRESSING AND IMPORTANT ECOLOGICAL PROBLEM. WRITE THE CORRESPONDING LETTER BESIDE THE NUMBER '1' ON THE ECO TIME-BOMB. FOR EXAMPLE, IF YOU THINK THE HOLES IN THE OZONE LAYER ARE THE MOST URGENT ECO PROBLEM WRITE (A) NEXT TO NUMBER ONE. THEN WORK THROUGH THE REST OF THE LIST IN ORDER OF PRIORITY. YOU HAVE FOUR MINUTES FOR THIS EXERCISE.

(a) HOLES IN THE OZONE LAYER

(b) H₂uhOh! AC!D RAIN

(c) DANGER RADIOACTIVE WASTE

(d) LITTER

(e) EXTINCTION OF SPECIES

(f) GREENHOUSE EFFECT

MY CHOICE
1.
2.
3.
4.
5.
6.
7.
8.
9.
10.
11.
12.
13.
14.

GROUP CHOICE
1.
2.
3.
4.
5.
6.
7.
8.
9.
10.
11.
12.
13.
14.

(g) DESTRUCTION OF RAIN FOREST

(h) AIR POLLUTION

(i) DEPLETION OF NATURAL RESOURCES

(j) USE OF LANDFILLS TO DISPOSE HOUSEHOLD RUBBISH

(k) WATER POLLUTION

(L) HELP RISE IN SEA LEVELS

(m) RISE IN SIZE OF HUMAN POPULATION

(n) INAPPROPRIATE USE OF FERTILE LAND

A) Use of CFC gases in aerosols and fridges has caused holes to appear in layers of the upper atmosphere which help block out harmful rays of the sun.

B) Smoke and fumes from factories, power stations and cars are making snow, fog and mist acidic. This attacks and damages buildings. It damages and kills trees. It also affects crops and wildlife.

C) The nuclear power industry produces highly dangerous waste which will be radioactive for hundreds if not thousands of years to come.

D) Wasteful packaging and thoughtless littering means our streets are clogged with crisp packets, fag ends and drinks cans.

E) Humankind is reducing the natural habitat of a wide variety of plants and animals. This results in the extinction of species daily.

F) Exhaust fumes from cars, methane gas from animals and rice fields and CFC gases from aerosols have all contributed to the build up of the 'greenhouse effect' which could lead to major climatic changes.

G) Each year an area of rain forest the size of Wales is cut down and destroyed. Almost all the world's rain forest will disappear within 25 years at the current rate of tree felling.

H) Fumes from cars and factories pollute the air. In some cities like Mexico, the effect is worse on people's lungs than smoking 20 cigarettes a day.

I) Oil, gas minerals, hardwood and other resources are being plundered with little thought for future generations.

J) Instead of recycling household rubbish, most countries simply dump their mountains of rubbish in huge landfills. This can poison the local water supply and lead to a build-up of methane gas. It also uses up valuable land.

K) Agricultural pesticides and nitrate fertilisers have turned up in our drinking water. One effect could be a reduction in the fertility of men.

L) Climatic changes are resulting in a worldwide rise in sea levels. Low lying islands and coastal regions could disappear within the next 30 years unless sea defences are built now.

M) In large parts of the world the human population is growing very quickly. Some experts fear that the world will be unable to sustain the expected world population in 30 years unless contraception and family planning advice is made more widely available.

N) Land which could be growing food for the local population is all too often used to grow cash crops like sugar for export. In many countries, starving people could be fed if the land was used to grow food.

Book Three: Culture

Every young person is different. Each is a wonderfully unique mix of looks, brains and personality. And when young people are looked at together these different shapes and colours form patterns. A variety of forces are at work in our society, which affect the individual and corporate shape of the culture that surrounds and influences young people. If you work with young people, you are one of those forces!

As young people grow and develop the forces which have most influence over them as children – parent(s), brothers and sisters, teachers, the home environment, TV, computer games – are joined by other powerful forces.

This series of meetings is designed to help you to help young people to see who and what these forces are, and to analyse the power they may hold over them.

We all influence other people and in turn we are influenced by those around us. I hope this term-long series will help equip you to become a positive and provocative 'influencer' of the young people in your youth group or club.

READY-TO-USE-MEETING GUIDE

PUBLICITY PAGE

Get your meeting noticed by using the ready-to-photocopy artwork below to promote the first week of this term-long series of meetings. Simply add the details of venue and time and photocopy onto paper or thin coloured card. This image can be shrunk in size to use as a personal invite or expanded to poster size to pin onto a notice board at church, school, youth club etc.

THE 'INFLUENCERS'

MEETING AIM:
To help young people identify and analyse the dominant teenage culture and worldview and to introduce a series of meetings which will ask the questions: Who are the main influencers of teenage culture? How is youth culture manipulated and why? What aspects of the dominant worldview should the Christian stand against? How can young Christians live in modern society but not be contaminated by it?

MIND MOULDERS
(10-15 mins)
There are seven key forces which influence young people in different but important ways. Draw on a whiteboard/OHP screen the list below and ask your group members to identify the main ways that each group influences/has influenced the way they think, their values, attitudes and ambitions...

Family (eg opinions about right and wrong)
Big business (eg feeding materialistic consumerism)
Government (eg through laws and official statements which give or deny opportunities for wealth creation/aspirations)
Peer group/friends (eg influence behaviour)
School (eg sex education or lack of it)
Sport (eg aspiring to be like a sporting hero)
Media (eg influence clothes you wear)

Conclude this by saying that over the next few weeks we will be particularly looking at the way that the media in all its forms affects our thinking, culture, values and beliefs.

CULTURE VULTURE
(10 mins)
Make up your own quiz on youth culture based on your own knowledge, teen magazines, video clips from popular films, teenage TV, etc. Check out the regular 'Street Cred' quiz in YOUTH**WORK** magazine for more ideas on the sorts of questions to set. Be sure to include a mixture of easy and tricky questions.

WHAT IS CULTURE?
(1 min)
A culture is a particular form, stage or type of civilisation. It defines the way a society or particular group of people think or behave. For example, our society has a monogomous cultural attitude towards sexual relationships.

CULTURE SHAPERS
(10-15 mins)
Photocopy and hand out copies of the Culture Shapers box opposite, plus pens. Allow five minutes for it to be completed then compare results and get people to read out their arguments for what they listed as number one media culture-shaper.

CULTURE CHAT
(15 mins)
This section is crucial and you need to think through the likely responses to the statements in order to facilitate a good discussion. Try to steer rather than dominate the discussion, allowing dissenting voices to make their point.
Discuss:
● What sort of opinions and values does the media communicate and how?
● Do you think people are aware of the fact that the media is influencing them?
● Do people generally resist media pressure or influence (eg to buy Wazzo because it washes whiter), do they give in to it straight away, or is it a gradual wearing-away process?
● If you watch lots of TV programmes which present pre-marital sex as the normal way to behave is it likely to affect your own opinions on the subject?

CULTURE CHAT
(10 mins)
Try reading out the following two Bible readings from the excellent new paraphrase *The Message*.

John 17:14-16.
'I gave them [the disciples] your word; the godless world hated them because of it, because they didn't join the world's ways, just as I didn't join the world's ways. I'm not asking you to take them out of the world, but that you guard them from the Evil One. They are no more defined by the world than I am defined by the world.'

EXPLAIN: that Jesus prays to God asking him to protect and help his disciples. Having spent three years with them Jesus is about to go through the big test of the trial and crucifixion - but he seems more concerned for his followers than himself. Emphasise that Jesus wants his followers to stay in contact with the world, without getting contaminated by the world's ways and culture. Some Christians have chosen to withdraw from the world (for example in monasteries) to help them focus on God and worship him. It may be easier to be close to God that way but Jesus makes it clear to his followers that he wants them to keep in contact with the world.

2 Corinthians 10:2-5.
'The world is unprincipled. It's dog-eat-dog out there! The world doesn't fight fair. But we don't live or fight our battles that way - never have and never will. The tools of our trade aren't for marketing or manipulation, but they are for demolishing that entire massively corrupt culture. We use our powerful God-tools for smashing warped philosophies, tearing down barriers erected against the truth of God, fitting every loose thought and emotion and impulse into the structure of life shaped by Christ.'

EXPLAIN: that Paul writes these instructions to the church in Corinth, one of the hardest places for a Christian to live 2,000 years ago. Corinth was a large seaport and notorious for its brothels, permissive lifestyle and mixture of religions and ideas. If you read Paul's two letters to the Corinthians that have survived to this day (he almost certainly wrote others) it is clear that the Christians were struggling not to let the culture of the non-Christians in the city pollute the church. The dilemma is that we need to understand and know the dominant culture so that we can function each day and communicate with non-Christians, but without getting sucked in so that we start living our lives according to the rules of their culture instead of God's way. Paul encourages the Corinthian believers that through the power of Christ they can resist and fight back against the corrupt culture they live in. We also can be encouraged by knowing that Jesus both understands how tough it is to be a Christian today, *and* he is praying for us and wanting us to overcome those difficulties.

Sum up by using this visual illustration, or come up with some other parable or picture story. Keep it brief - a maximum three minutes, so that you make a quick impact, and then stop while you are still winning!

Hold up a glass tumbler and fill it one-third full with water. **SAY:** 'This clean water symbolises our lives when we become Christians. We are clean and pure. But we live in a society which, like Corinth in the first century, has a twisted and partly evil culture. This drips into us and if we are not careful it changes us.' At this point slowly put a few drops of food colouring into the water and swirl the glass around so the

CULTURE SHAPERS

Key media channels help shape the culture of young people. From the list below put them in a 1 to 7 listing in the order of their influence. For example if you think music is the biggest single media influence on teenage culture put a '1' beside it.

.... **Books, magazines & newspapers**

.... **Film and video**

.... **Sport and recreation**

.... **Computer games**

.... **Music**

.... **Television**

In no more than 60 words explain why you think you are right about the number one media culture-shaper. Imagine that you are arguing with someone who has put something else in the top spot.

---

colour mixes into the water.

'We stop being pure and we get infected by the values and thoughts of the non-Christian culture around us.' Then hold up another tumbler which is already one-third full of cooking oil, pour the coloured water from the first glass into this one. The oil and coloured water should remain separate. Say: 'Jesus promises the Holy Spirit to all his followers to help them keep Christ's

lifestyle and values even when we are surrounded by an evil culture.'

Swirl the glass. The oil and water will appear to mix but will quickly separate again.

SAY: 'Even when we are under pressure God promises that we can remain in the world but resist the pressure to conform to its standards. When we do that we make a

powerful witness by being different; not cranky or weird, but strong, choosing not to go along with the crowd.' Hold up the glass tumbler again - and say: 'During the next few weeks we are going to take a closer look at some of the things which are affecting the culture of our country and look at ways we can have fun and be ourselves without getting sucked into the down-side of our culture.'

HAPPINESS IS...

MEETING AIM
To highlight the difference between the value system of Jesus and our modern culture.

CALL MY BLUFF
(10 mins)
Use this popular TV quiz game from the 80s to introduce this week's meeting.

Write out onto a postcard-size piece of card the three definitions of the word 'hedonism' below. Choose three members of the group who are confident and good readers and give them one card each. Explain that of the three definitions two are 'bluffs'(incorrect), but that they should be read out in a convincing way, so that as many of the group as possible will decide one of these is the correct definition. The person who has the true definition has the opposite task: to convince the group that he/she is trying to 'bluff' them.

HEDONISM
A medical condition caused by drinking a very large amount of alcohol in a short period of time. Frequent hedonism, which is sometimes called 'binge drinking' can lead to alcoholic poisoning, liver damage or heart failure. **(BLUFF)**

HEDONISM
The word originates from the Latin word 'heed' and characterises the attitude of someone who is naturally cautious. People who dislike taking risks are therefore practising 'hedonism' and are sometimes called 'hedonistic' as a result. **(BLUFF)**

HEDONISM
A teaching of some ancient Greek philosophers who believed that the main goal in life should be seeking pleasure and indulging one's own desires. **(TRUE)**

Once the definitions have been read out twice to the group ask for a show of hands on each definition to discover who thinks what. Finally, read through again the correct definition of hedonism and explain that for many people today the pursuit of personal happiness is their ambition and purpose for living.

HAPPINESS IS...
(15 mins)
For this game you will need an old-fashioned brass lamp or something similar, which looks a bit like the lamp from the tale of Aladdin. Get everyone in a circle and then read out the statement below;

> **'Happiness is**
> *having parents that love you*
> *being as well dressed as anyone*
> *in your crowd*
> *having your own room*
> *getting the telephone call you've*
> *been waiting for*
> *being popular*
> *having parents that don't fight*
> *something I don't have.'*
>
> Signed 15 and unhappy

Then hand the first person in the circle the lamp and say: 'Imagine that a genie appeared and told you he could grant you three wishes which would make you happy. What would they be? Remember they should be wishes that once granted will make you very happy.' The first person then says what their three wishes for happiness would be. Have someone listing the wishes on an OHP or whiteboard. Once everyone has had a turn with the lamp quickly recap and reveal which were the most popular wishes.

HAPPY QUOTES
(3 mins)
Read out or write onto OHP or whiteboard the following quotes about happiness.

'Happiness is having a sauna then relaxing in a bath with a music tape playing.'
George Michael (singer)

'I never took pleasure in earning money. Money is not necessarily related to happiness. Maybe it is related to unhappiness.'
John Paul Getty (multi-millionaire)

'I think whoever said money can't buy happiness simply hadn't found out where to go shopping.'
Bo Derek (actress)

'Money brings some happiness, but after a certain point it just brings more money.'
Neil Simon (singer)

'God gives wisdom, knowledge, and happiness to those who please him.'
Ecclesiastes 2:26

'The first requisite for the happiness of the people is the abolition of religion.'
Karl Marx (philosopher)

'You have made us for yourself and our hearts are restless until they find their rest in you.'
St Augustine (theologian)

HAPPINESS JESUS-STYLE
(20-25 mins)
The longest talk that Jesus gave that the gospels recorded is called the Sermon on the Mount (Matthew 5:1-7:29). In it Jesus talks about how we can be happy. But Jesus' list of 'happiness is', commonly called the beatitudes, is very different from most people's. According to Jesus people who mourn can be happy because at that moment they can experience God's closeness. Get people in pairs then hand out copies of the sheet opposite and a pen to each pair. Explain that they should write down the exact opposite beside each of the statements from Matthew 5 (see example). They have 10 minutes to complete as much of sheet as they can with their anti-beatitudes. Get feedback afterwards from two or three different pairs on each anti-beatitude. This should illustrate that the value system of today's culture is almost the opposite of Jesus'.

SAY: 'Most people think that happiness depends on them being OK, and their lifestyle is built around making sure they get material and sexual pleasure. But is having good health, money and people who love you the way to true happiness? Jesus taught that true happiness comes when you are close to God and when you care about the things God cares about.' At this point I recommend that you read Matthew 5:1-12 from *The Message* a modern paraphrase of the New Testament written by Eugene Peterson (Navpress/Scripture Press).

Allow the young people to come back at you with questions or an alternative viewpoint here. The idea that people who are mourning, humble, pure in heart, and so on, will be happy freaks most people. Help them to understand what Jesus is talking about. You may also want to point your group in the direction of the four Bible passages below which counter the idea that Christians can't have fun or live happy and fulfilled lives.

- John 10:10
- John 15:9,11
- 1 Timothy 6:17
- 1 John 2:15-17

Happiness is –
JESUS STYLE

Read each of the sayings of Jesus from the first part of the Sermon on the Mount on the left side and then come up with the exact opposite to write in the right side column (see example below).

HAPPY are those who know they are Spiritually poor; the Kingdom of Heaven belongs to them

HAPPY are those who don't realise they are spiritually poor; they get all they want in this world.

HAPPY are those who mourn; God will comfort them!

....
....
....

HAPPY are those who are humble; they will receive what God has promised!

....
....
....

HAPPY are those whose greatest desire is to do what God requires; God will satisfy them fully!

....
....
....

HAPPY are those who are merciful to others; God will be merciful to them!

....
....
....

HAPPY are the pure in heart; they will see God!

....
....
....

HAPPY are those who work for peace; God will call them his children!

....
....
....

HAPPY are those who are persecuted because they do what God requires; the Kingdom of heaven belongs to them!

....
....
....

Matthew 5:3-10 (Good News Bible)

READ ALL ABOUT IT

MEETING AIM
To encourage young people to analyse and investigate the content and ethos of popular newspapers and magazines, and to reveal that almost every publication has a message or underlying philosophy it wants to communicate. To suggest that constant exposure to stories about evil can desensitise and pollute the mind.

HEADLINE NEWS
(10 mins)
Buy at least eight well known daily newspapers (*The Sun, Daily Mirror/Record, Daily Express, Today, Daily Mail, The Scotsman, Daily Telegraph, The Guardian, The Independent, The Times*) on the same day, preferably not more than seven days prior to using this meeting plan. Photocopy onto A3 paper the front pages and keep these safe to use as a reference for the correct answers. Then cut the mastheads with the title of each newspaper from the rest of the front page so that you end up with eight mastheads and eight front pages. Number the mastheads 1 to 8, then mix up the front pages and affix a letter *a* to *h*.

Before the meeting begins stick the mastheads and front pages onto a wall or chalkboard. As the young people arrive hand out paper and pens and explain they have to match the masthead to the correct front page.

At the end of the game read out the answers and/or show them the photocopied complete front pages and introduce the theme of the meeting.

WHO READS WHAT?
(15 mins)
Conduct a mini-survey of reading habits among your group to discover what if any newspaper they regularly read, and what if any magazine(s) they regularly read. Collect the results and write them up on an OHP or white/chalkboard, then compare them to the statistics below. Ask the young people to list on paper and then report back, or discuss in small groups, why *The Sun, Viz, Just Seventeen, Smash Hits* and computer magazines are so popular with young people. What is it about them that is appealing?

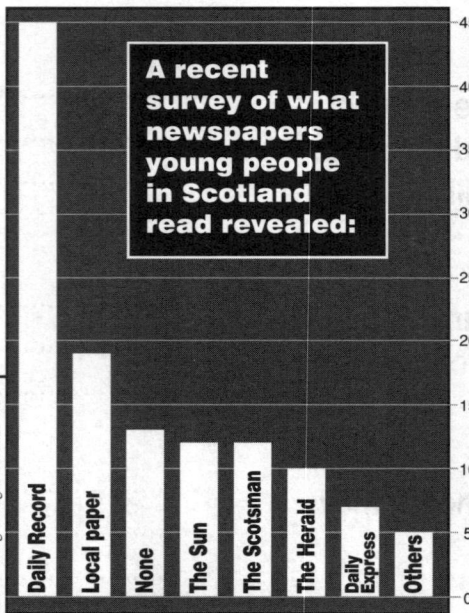

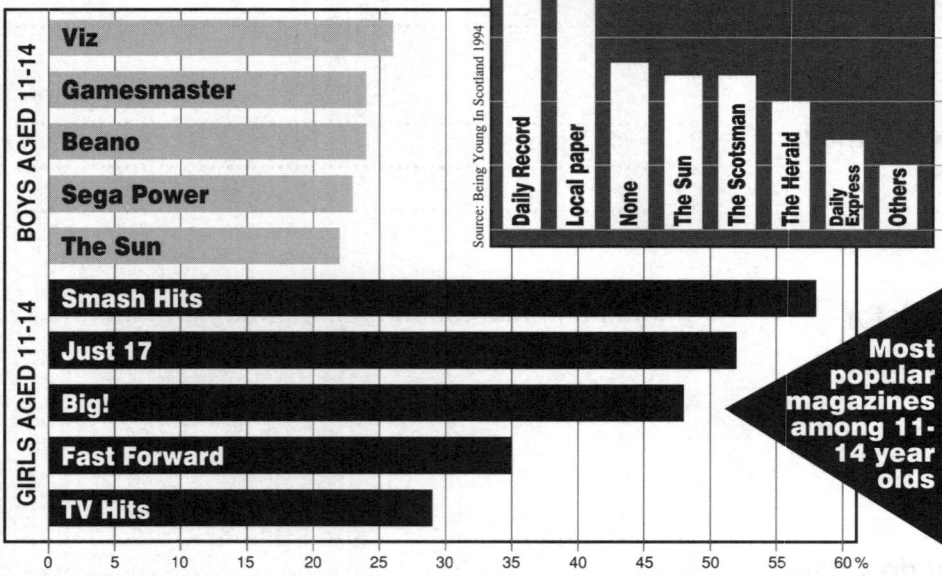

A recent survey of what newspapers young people in Scotland read revealed:

Source: Being Young In Scotland 1994

[Bar chart — newspapers read by young people in Scotland: Daily Record (~19), Local paper (~14), None (~11), The Sun (~11), The Scotsman (~10), The Herald (~8), Daily Express (~6), Others]

[Bar chart — Boys aged 11-14 (Source: BMRB Youth TGI 1993): Viz, Gamesmaster, Beano, Sega Power, The Sun. Girls aged 11-14: Smash Hits, Just 17, Big!, Fast Forward, TV Hits]

Most popular magazines among 11-14 year olds

DIGGING DEEPER
(5-10 mins)
In small groups, or working as individuals, hand out copies of a tabloid newspaper and ask the groups or individuals to list the story contents in note form. For example, page 1: Scandal of politician and call girl; man arrested after three people are murdered. Then do the same with the contents page of a popular teen magazine (not including computer or sports titles).
Tell everyone to keep their lists for later.

TRUE STORIES
(10 mins)
ASK: 'What is the most revolting thing you have ever eaten? It could be something you ate by accident, like a fly in a bowl of soup, or something you chose to eat like snails.' After everyone has given an answer and the laughter and screams have died down, make the point that we tend to be careful about eating things that will make us feel sick. People are also becoming increasingly concerned about pollution in the air they breathe, the water they drink, and the seawater they bathe in at the beach.

Emphasise that everyone naturally tries to avoid foul, contaminated, polluted or dirty things getting into our bodies.

MIND POLLUTION
(25 mins)
Read together Romans 1:20-32. Read it through slowly - preferably twice. Then:
● Ask if people have the same attitude towards polluting their minds as their bodies.
● Ask everyone to take another look at the list of newspaper or magazine contents which they wrote up earlier. Some of the stories may be educational, informative and helpful. But often the newspapers are swamped with sad, brutal, violent stories, with the tabloids and teen magazines also giving a lot of space to 'gossip' about film, soap or music 'stars'. Teen mags and tabloids also tend to contain a high content of sex and sexual behaviour.
● Pose the question: If we keep reading about murders, rape, violence, adultery, jealousy, sexual promiscuity, sexual perversions, materialistic attitudes, betrayal, double standards, corruption etc, will this deaden our senses and make us less sensitive to other people's pain?
● Ask whether people think exposure to 'bad' news has a temporary or lasting effect?
● Ask what qualifications and life experience people think a newspaper or teen magazine agony aunt or uncle should have? Make the point that Philip Hodson, who was the agony uncle on BBC 1's Going Live, a popular Saturday morning children's programme in 1992, and also advised teens in an agony column in the *News of the World*, was a former editor of a sex magazine. While Nick Fisher, agony uncle in *Just Seventeen* admitted in a *Daily Mail* article that his own teenage years were 'somewhat of a disaster. I fought with my parents and got expelled from school. I was

Just Sixteen ½

obnoxious.' Fisher's first marriage ended in divorce when he was 26. Often these so called 'experts' have made a mess of their lives and yet they advise millions of others. Discuss.

READ: 2 Timothy 3:2-5.
Explain that this letter from Paul warns his friend Timothy about people who love only themselves and money. Timothy was living and working for the church in Ephesus when Paul wrote to him. Paul was very aware that this city was notorious for the self-centred and materialistic lifestyle of its citizens. That is why many Christians feel Paul's advice to Timothy about avoiding the influence of evil, money-loving people (v5) also applies to Christians today who live in materialistic countries like the USA, Japan and Western Europe including the British Isles. Some people say this advice can also apply to other forms of 'influence' apart from actually being in the company of evil people. Could this apply to what we read? Discuss.

AND NOW FOR THE GOOD NEWS
(10-15 mins)

Divide everyone into single-sex groups of two or three. Hand out enlarged A4 copies of the sheets opposite and felt-tipped pens. Give the groups of girls the *Just 16´* cover and the boys *The Stun* and ask them to think up, write and design front covers for this magazine/newspaper.

The cover should include a drawn picture, photo or illustration, plus headlines and details of the contents in the typical style of a teen mag or tabloid paper. Give them five minutes then hand out a second identical blank cover and ask them to choose only positive good news stories. There should be no intrusive reporting, no dodgy gossip, no sensationalist headlines, only hard facts, helpful and moral information.

End the session by comparing covers and asking which cover they found the easiest to design and why. Conclude by underlining that every newspaper and magazine has a philosophy and a bias. We need to be careful about accepting as true everything we read. Christians believe the Bible is the guideline by which all other advice and points of view should be measured and compared.

The Stun

SQUARE EYES

MEETING AIM
It would be easy to come across as negative and condemning on this subject. The objective of this meeting is to encourage young people to think about what they watch, to evaluate a programme and to be more selective in their viewing habits.

TELLY ADDICTS
(20 mins)
Play a version of this popular BBC TV programme hosted by Noel Edmonds. Ask for volunteers to make up two teams of up to four in each. Use short video clips from programmes, pictures of TV personalities cut out of TV listings magazines, recordings of programme theme tunes, and TV trivia quizbooks to collect an interesting range of questions to discover who is your youth group/club champion telly addict.

TELLY WATCH
(10-15 mins)
Hand out copies of the TV set worksheet opposite and ask the group to list their top 10 favourite TV programmes. Then get the young people to read out from 10 to 1 their TV choices to come up with an overall youth group/club checklist of most popular shows. The easiest way to do this is to award a programme listed as number 10 with one point, number 9 with two points, and so on up to number 1 with 10 points. The programmes with the most points represent your group's favourites. It will also be interesting and fun to ask everyone to choose one programme that they really detest and to say why they dislike it so much.

TELLY STATS
(3 mins)
Read out the following statistics:
● According to the British Audience Research Board children between four and 15 in the UK spent, on average, just over 19 hours a week watching television in 1993.
● The most popular programmes are the 'soaps' *Neighbours, Home and Away, Eastenders* and *Coronation Street*. One in five watches *Grange Hill*.
● Research from the Youth Times Group Index shows that two thirds of 11 to 14-year-olds have a TV in their room.
● The Government's own report 'Special Focus on Children 1994' produced by the Central Statistical Office estimates that children and younger teens watch an average of 20 hours of television a week.
● By the age of 14, the average American has seen 11,000 murders on television.
● British statistics are less dramatic, but the body count is still alarmingly high.
● A 1992 analysis of a typical day of TV, commissioned by the listing magazine TV Guide counted 10 acts of violence per hour. (*The Independent* 25 October 1993).
● In 1984 a Parliamentary Group Video Enquiry revealed viewing figures based on a survey of 7 to 16-year-old children in England and Wales. 18.4% had seen *The Evil Dead*; 17.8% had seen *Zombie Flesh Eater*; 15.9% had seen *The Living Dead* and 15.8% had seen *The Bogey Man*. These videos include knifing, raping, torturing and dismembering.

TELLY TALK
(25 mins)
In an interview published in the *Radio Times*, Noel Edmonds says:'A significant percentage of social ills are caused by that box in the corner. There's a lot I don't want to expose my daughters (aged 11, six and three) to, and a lot of views are expressed which are not of any great value to society.' From the moment his daughters could read, he made them aware of programme listings. 'We won't have them sitting in front of mindless cartoons and don't have the soaps in the house at all.' He adds that there is a fight to see who can turn off the television first if the *Neighbours* signature tune is heard. 'It's light weight rubbish which doesn't give an accurate perspective of life - I'd rather they watched *Baywatch* - and I'm fed up with people arguing all the time in *EastEnders*.'

Ask your young people:
● Do you agree with Noel Edmonds' opinion of soaps?
● Do you watch a specific programme and then turn the TV off, or do you tend to watch whatever is on?
● Which TV programmes do you consider are good to watch?
● Which TV programmes do you think are harmful or bad to watch?
● Do you think watching TV affects the way people think and behave (eg in the case of the murder of James Bulger)?
● What about the religious programmes on TV like *Songs of Praise*? Are these programmes creative, uplifting, entertaining? What should they be like?
● Do you think you would spend your time differently if you didn't watch any TV?

READ: 1 Thessalonians 5:21; Philippians 4:8 and ask how we should we apply these verses to what TV we watch.

TELLY OPTIONS
1) Watch a TV programme together as a group and then discuss it afterwards. Encourage the young people to critique what they watch rather than swallow it whole.

2) Challenge your youngsters to go on a television famine - going without any TV for 24 hours, 48 hours, or even a week. This could be a valuable exercise if everyone gets involved. You could decide in advance how you will spend the TV-free time.

3) Ask each member of your group to write a letter to the controller of the BBC, ITV or Channel 4, or to one of the viewers' feedback programmes like the BBC's 'Points of View'. They should identify which programmes they like or think are well made, and identify areas where they feel young people are poorly represented. Do they feel children's and youth TV programmes are overall good, bad or indifferent? Get their voice heard.

4) Challenge your group members to keep a TV diary for a week. They should jot down in the diary the time and details of programmes they watch. Ask them also to write down comments about the content of the programmes, eg was it entertaining, boring, funny, educational? They should conclude by explaining why they kept watching the programme or why they turned off the TV. At the end of a week ask everyone to report back and compare their diary entries. This exercise tends to encourage more discerning viewing.

CONCLUSION
When you tie up the meeting be careful not to condemn TV. Instead emphasise the good things about TV; that it can be relaxing, a good source of information, and that it can be fun. But also encourage the young people to evaluate carefully what they watch, how much time they spend watching TV, and challenge them to be more discerning about what they watch. They could write down their own TV guidelines for what they watch and when they switch off.

SQUARE

EYES

1. ....
2. ....
3. ....
4. ....
5. ....
6. ....
7. ....
8. ....
9. ....
10. ....

The TV programme I dislike most is

....

....

I can't stand this programme because

....

....
....
....
....
....
....
....
....

RAVE N' ROCK

MEETING AIM

To help the group become more discerning about the lyrical content and lifestyle values they absorb from popular music. To help them see that music is a neutral medium and can be used to promote a wide range of good or bad messages and lifestyles. This meeting requires a fair amount of pre-planning. If you know little or nothing about contemporary music you will find it helpful to have someone who knows the difference between black metal and ragga present.

LYRIC QUIZ
(10 mins)

Buy the latest copy of *Smash Hits* magazine which will contain the lyrics of some current chart songs. Copy a couple of lines from the lyrics of a song onto a postcard-size piece of card and number the card. You will need at least ten songs, and therefore ten cards.

Before the meeting begins pin the cards onto the walls of the meeting room. As the group arrive hand out pens and paper and tell them they must identify as many song titles, plus artists/bands as they can. Keep the game running until every one has arrived. Then award record tokens for the winner(s).

WHO LISTENS TO WHAT
(5 mins)

Hand out copies of the sheet opposite and a pen to every person, then ask them to complete the exercise. If you have time get them to list as many bands beside each musical genre that they can.

TOP OF THE POPS
(10 mins)

Ask individuals to say who their favourite band/artist is. Phone some people beforehand to discover what they will say so you can play a sample track from the band. This should be done in a fun way. You can cerainly expect some difference of opinion and a few boos and whistles if you play Take That!

BITS N' PIECES
(10 mins)

Prepare beforehand a cassette tape of about ten clips from chart/dance music - the clips should last no longer than 10 seconds. Hand out pens and paper to everyone and play each clip with a very short pause between songs. Then play back the song clips and give the correct answers. Award one point for the song title and one point for the band/artist. If you're feeling generous award a record token to the winner(s) and/or a Christian music tape of someone your kids will like eg Carmen, DC Talk, Worldwide Message Tribe. Alternatively you could play this game by rough-editing bits and pieces from music videos and playing onto a large-screen TV or video projector.

GOOD OR BAD?
(15 mins)

ASK:

1) 'How do you decide if a song is good or bad?'

2) 'If a song has racist, violent, explicitly sexual or crude lyrics should a Christian listen to it?'

3) 'Can the lyrics of a song affect a person's mood or beliefs?'

Expect to get a range of views and some fiery discussion over these questions. Please do not jump in with both feet and loudly express your views. Allow everyone to have their say and be open and honest. Do not judgementally criticise other views, but simply state what you think and why. Make the point that rock, rap, or jungle music, as a style or genre of music, is not good or bad in itself. Music is a neutral medium, but it can be made good or evil. The lifestyle and example of the performers, and the lyrical content, are key factors in determining the direction and influence the music will have.

THE BIBLE AND MUSIC
(10 mins)

Check out the following Scriptures and ask the group to discuss what they have to say about music.

- Philippians 1:27-28
- Colossians 2:6-8
- Titus 1:15
- Psalms 150

OPTIONAL EXTRAS

VIDEO VERDICT

Play a variety of Christian and secular music videos and get the group to identify positive and negative messages and influences the band and that particular song make. Talk together and attempt to reach a consensus decision about some bands which are unhelpful because of their anti-Christian lifestyle message.

WORSHIP

Conclude the session by using Psalms 150 or other Scriptures as a trigger for worship. You could use recorded worship tapes or get a worship group from your church to lead the group in an extended time of worship which focuses on the positive way that music can help us worship God.

MINI-CONCERT

Invite a local Christian band to do a mini-concert and then be interviewed about their faith and the way they use music to spread the good news.

METAL

MOD

TEDS

DRaW a LiNE BETWEEN THE CHaRaCTER and the type of MUSiC LiSTENED 2

New Age. Crusties

RAP

JUNGLE

REGGAE

Punk

SELLING POWER

MEETING AIM
To examine the powerful influence adverts have over us, and how in turn Christians are adverts (good or bad) for the Christian faith.

AWARENESS TEST
(10 mins)

Ask everyone to stand and close their eyes. Ask questions about things in the room which require yes or no answers, eg 'Are the curtains orange? Is Jane wearing a baseball hat?' Hands up for yes. Call out the names of those who are wrong and ask them to sit down. Continue with those left standing until there is a winner.

ASK: How aware are we of adverts? All the time we are being bombarded with adverts and many of these leave impressions in our sub-conscious mind. The manufacturers who sell a product want us to identify with it, so when we go shopping we see a familiar product - their product - and buy it. But do we really take these adverts in, or is it a case of 'in one ear and out the other?'

Discuss this question.

NAME THAT AD
(10 mins)

Prepare beforehand a video of TV adverts, being careful to miss out the bits where the brand name is mentioned or shown. Split into groups of twos or threes and hand out pens and paper to each group. Play the video through and ask the groups to identify the products

OR

Tear out ads from magazines and cut out the brand name and logo. Write a number on the corner of each ad, then pin or stick them on the wall or whiteboard and ask the group to identify the product or manufacturer being advertised.

SAY: 'Research has shown that, even when people know that adverts are trying to persuade them to buy something they don't need, they are still influenced by them.'

WHICH ONE'S BEST
(5 mins)

Hand out copies of the cartoon opposite and a pen or pencil to each member of your group. Ask them to circle the two most effective forms of advertising and put a triangle around the two least effective. Allow two minutes for this exercise, then get feedback and reasons why they think some media for adverts are more powerful and appealing than others.

AD CHAT
(10-15 mins)

Ask everyone to share briefly what their favourite advert of all time is and why.

Analyse some of the adverts from the earlier 'name that ad' game. Unpack the message behind the ad, eg this cola will give you life, this bodyspray will get you boyfriends. Some of the messages are subtle, some, like most perfume ads, are blatant.

Sum up by saying: 'We need to be careful what we take in and believe. What adverts say can affect our view of life and the world. In the same way, what Christians say and do affects what others think of Jesus/the church/youth club/group.'

BIBLE HUNT
(10 mins)

The adverts want us to be identified with their products in what we wear, buy etc. God wants Christians to be identified with Jesus. Check out these verses:

Mark 5:19; Acts 1:8; 2 Timothy 1:8a; 1 Peter 3:15.

IDENTIFICATION
(10 mins)

The disciples identified with Jesus by wearing simple clothes/carrying no money or food/doing his work. Discuss: In what ways can we be identified with Jesus in the modern world?

(One point to bring out is John 13:34-35.)

D.I.Y. ADVERT
(15 mins)

In groups of three or four, ask people to brainstorm a 30-second advert for your youth group. As well as a script, they should come up with a rough storyboard. A storyboard is a collection of outline pictures which show what will be in the frame of the camera when shooting the video. Next week, hire or borrow enough video cameras for each group to have 45 minutes shooting time. Supply popcorn and soft drinks for the end of the evening, when the group relax around the TV and watch each others' adverts.

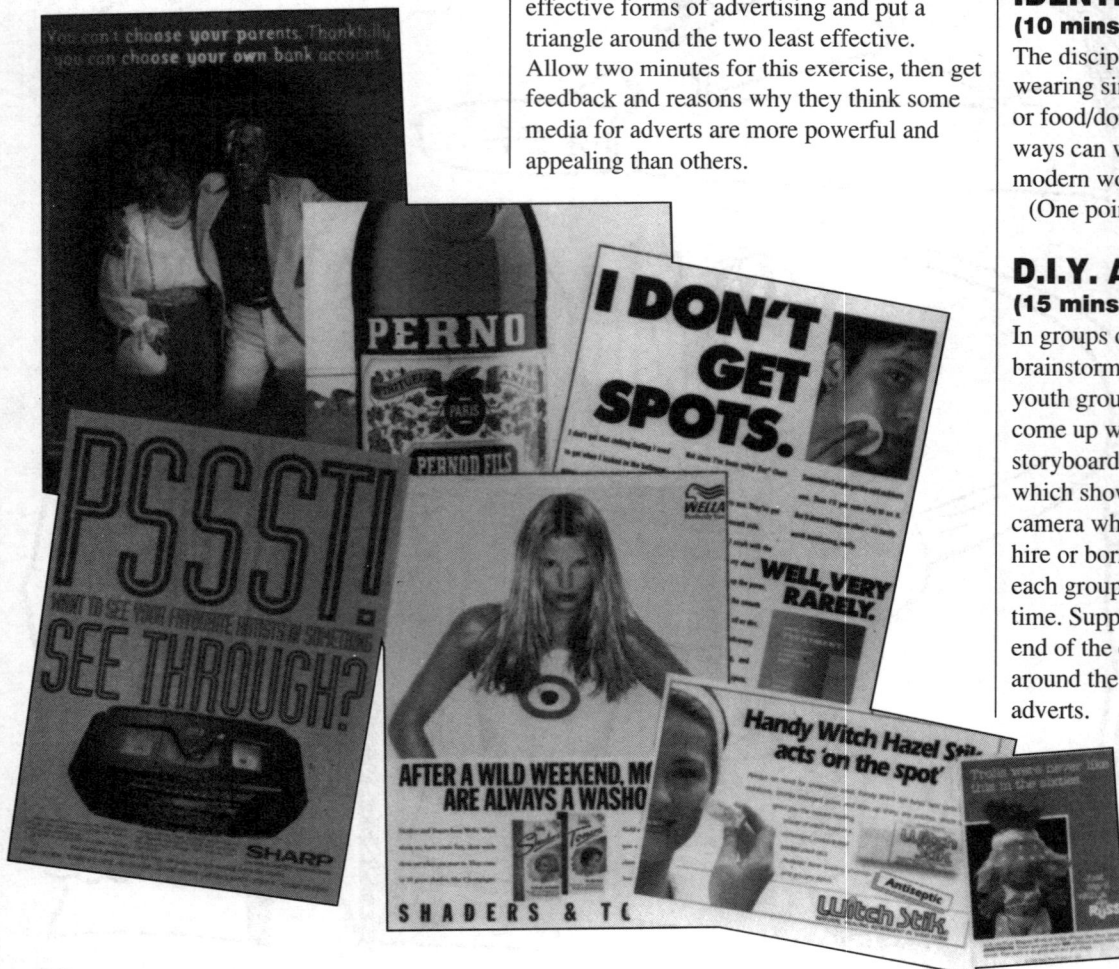

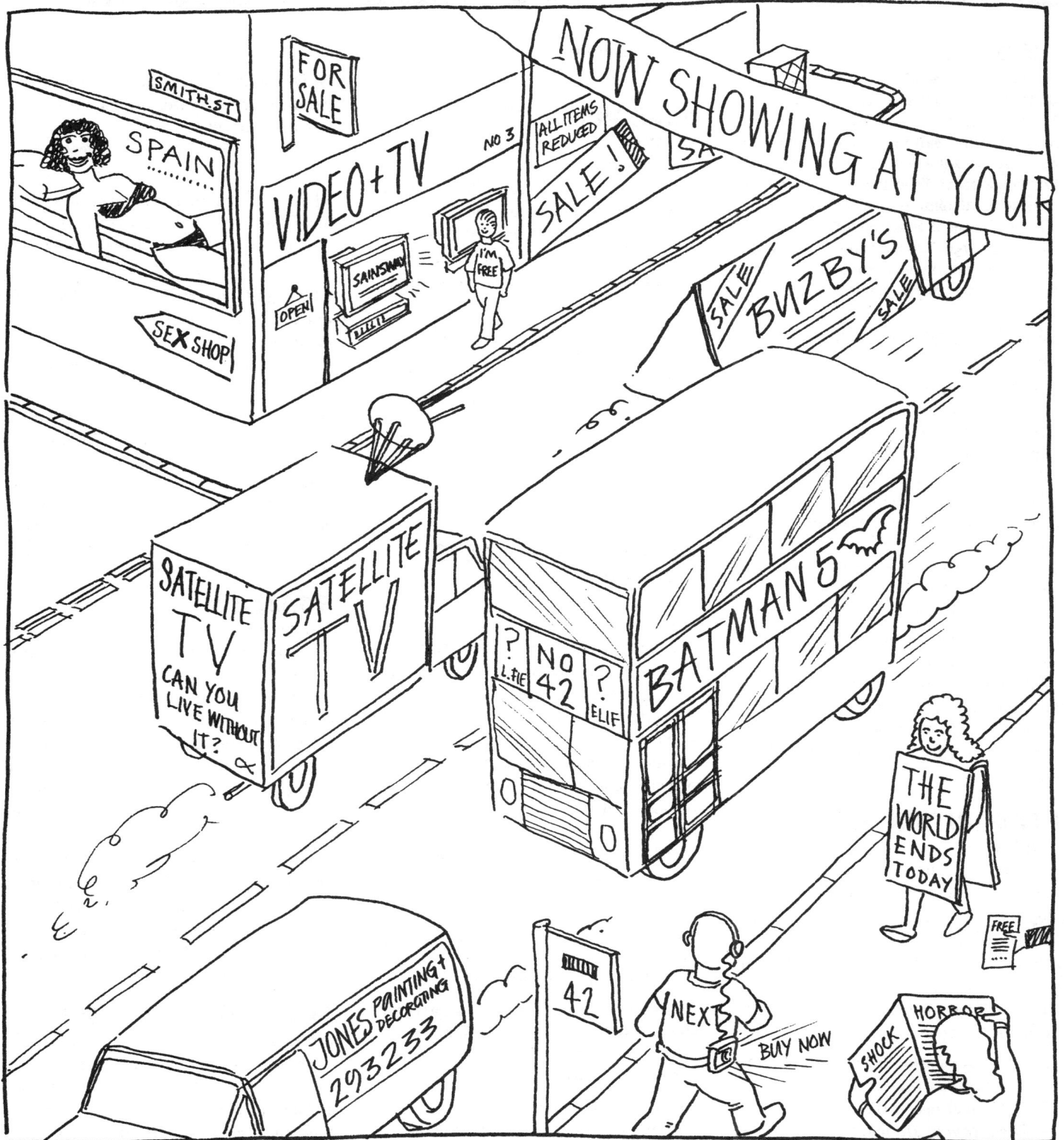

ALL·THE·WORLDS·A·PAGE

WHICH MEANS OF ADVERTISING IS THE MOST EFFECTIVE? TV, HOARDINGS, ADS, MAGAZINES? LOOK AT THE CARTOON + CIRCLE THE 2 MEANS OF ADVERTISING YOU THINK WORK THE BEST, ARE THE MOST MEMORABLE + PERSUASIVE. THEN DRAW A TRIANGLE AROUND THE 2 WHICH ARE THE LEAST EFFECTIVE, MEMORABLE + PERSUASIVE.

BOOZE UP

MEETING AIM

Educate about the effects of alcohol. Underline the level of recognition that breweries have achieved for their alcohol brands through saturation advertising, and to examine the arguments breweries make for drinking alcohol. To examine what the Bible says about alcohol. To consider the harmful effects of alcohol abuse on individuals and society at large. You may need to add to or adapt this material according to the specific stance on alcohol your church takes.

SILLY CONFESSIONS
(10 mins)

Use this activity as an icebreaker and a good introduction to the overall meeting theme. Ask everyone to tell the story of 'the silliest thing they have ever done'. Start the ball rolling by speaking first. Make sure, as others share their stories, that any laughter is at the situation and not at the person telling the story.

You may find that one of the stories is about a silly thing done while under the influence of alcohol. If not, link into the theme by saying that one of the effects that alcohol has on the body is to reduce inhibitions. As a result people often do silly things if they drink too much - things which in the cold light of day, they would never normally do. This is just one of the effects of alcohol...

RECOGNITION QUIZ
(5 mins)

Hand out paper and pens and ask individuals to list the brand of booze the following slogans refer to. Use this game to illustrate the level of recognition that brewers can achieve through saturation advertising. Their product gets lodged in our minds. Hand out a packet of wine gums to the person(s) with the highest score!

1) *Australians wouldn't give a xxxx for anything else* (Castlemaine 4X)
2) *The amber nectar* (Fosters)
3) *The cream of Manchester* (Boddingtons)
4) *I'm not bitter* (Murphy's)
5) *The right one* (Martini)
6) *I bet he drinks...* (Carling Black Label)
7) *The genuine article* (Budweiser)
8) *Refreshes the parts other beers cannot reach* (Heineken)
9) *In Paris you drop the 'd'* (Pernod)
10) *Pure Genius* (Guinness)
11) *Britain's biggest bottled beer* (Newcastle Brown Ale)
12) *Probably the best lager in the world* (Carlsberg)

REASONS WHY?
(5 mins)

Ask your group to come up with reasons why young people drink alcohol. If they are slow to make suggestions, encourage comment by outlining some of the typical situations where young people drink (at parties, hanging around on street corners with friends, alone at home). List their comments on a whiteboard, flip chart or OHP. Be careful not to make any judgemental comments or slip into 'preach' mode at this stage; what you are doing is compiling a list of reasons. Hopefully your group will come up with a long list which should include: way to relax, Dutch courage, peer pressure, to get drunk, availability, relatively inexpensive.

ALCOHOL: THE FACTS
(5-8 mins)

Get everyone to stand in the middle of the room. Designate one wall of the room 'true' and the opposite 'false'. Group members have to decide whether the statements you read out are true or false and then move to the appropriate side of the room after each statement. This exercise also raises questions of the influence of peer pressure on behaviour - it's hard to be the only person on one side of the room. If the room does not allow very much movement, you could adapt by sitting for 'true', and standing for 'false', or alternatively simply make it a pen and paper exercise.

1) **Alcohol is a stimulant drug, it peps you up.**
(FALSE - alcohol is a depressant.)

2) **Eating before and during a party will slow down the effects of alcohol.**
(TRUE - food in the stomach slows down the absorption of alcohol into the bloodstream.)

3) **Black coffee sobers you up.**
(FALSE - the caffeine may keep you awake but only time will sober you up.)

4) **When you go to the toilet most alcohol passes out in urine.**
(FALSE - only about 6-10% of alcohol is expelled in urine, sweat or breath, the rest has to be broken down (oxidised) by the liver working at a rate of about one unit of alcohol per hour.)

5) **Mixing alcohol with another drug can be very dangerous.**
(TRUE - the results can be very unpredictable and sometimes fatal, like River Phoenix).

6) **One pint of lager does not affect a person's driving skills or chances of having an accident.**
(FALSE - accident risk increases after the very first drink especially in young people.)

7) **Alcohol drunk during pregnancy is passed on to the baby in the womb.**
(TRUE - this increases the chance of deformed, retarded or low weight babies.)

8) **Around a quarter of all convictions for murder involve people who had been drinking.**
(FALSE - the true figure is double that, around 50%!)

9) **Alcohol affects judgement, reflexes, vision and removes some inhibitions.**
(TRUE - alcohol acts on the brain like an anaesthetic. From the first drink self control and other functions are affected. It can also 'turn you on' sexually, but as Shakespeare said, 'alcohol provokes the desire but takes away the performance' [*Macbeth* Act 2 Scene 3].)

BOOZE-UP
(10-15 mins)

Hand out a copy of the poster sheet opposite to every member of your group, plus a selection of felt tipped pens. Ask them to design a poster for 'Booze-Up' lager which is brutally honest about the product, eg 'drink four bottles of this and it could make you vomit'. Allow five or 10 minutes for people to design and write their poster then get everyone to read them out.

Hold up a few lager or beer adverts from magazines which you have collected earlier. Unpack the glossy message of the ad (a drink for real men, the trendy drink, an all-American beer) and compare them to the Booze-Up posters.

BOOZE AND THE BIBLE
(15 mins)

In groups of two or three ask people to check out two of the Bible passages below and then be prepared to discuss them with everyone else. Make sure all the verses listed are covered by at least one group, if necessary ask the groups to study more than two Scripture passages.

Ask the groups to share what they have learned from the Bible passages. Discuss: Does Scripture contradict itself over drinking alcohol? (Some verses suggest it is a gift from God, others warn against drunkenness.) Help the young people to see that the Bible does not forbid drinking alcohol, but it is very clear that it forbids drunkenness. The Christian should always allow the Spirit of God to be in control, not spirit from a bottle! Also stress that in first-century Palestine there was no multi-million brewing industry investing huge amounts in advertising.

- **Genesis 27:28**
  (Wine, together with grain, stands for the good gifts of God)
- **Isaiah 5:11-12**
  (God was angry with the Jewish people for their evil ways: one of the reasons God was angry was their all-day drinking and partying which resulted in drunkenness.)

Psalm 104:13-15
  (Wine is listed alongside rain, plants, olive oil and bread as a good gift from God.)

Isaiah 28:7-8
  (Getting drunk results in confusion, God's prophets failed to hear accurately from God, and were unable to provide justice, the place was a shambles.)

John 2:1-11
  (Jesus' first miracle was to produce a large amount of best quality wine from water. Jesus was often criticised for eating and drinking with social outcasts.)

Ephesians 5:15-20
  (Christians should be controlled by the Holy Spirit, rather than alcohol.)

1 Timothy 3:8
  (Church leaders should not drink too much alcohol.)

Romans 14:21
  (It may be necessary to avoid alcohol altogether for the sake of weaker people.)

OPTIONAL EXTRAS

UNDER THE INFLUENCE

Ask a uniformed policeman to come and be interviewed about the effects of alcohol. Ask him/her to tell you about a typical Saturday night in the town centre and what happens when the pubs shut. How much domestic violence, vandalism, public disorder and other crime is directly related to the consumption of alcohol? How do people change when they drink? What about drinking and driving? The purpose of this interview is to underline the often very negative effects that drinking alcohol has on the individual, his/her family and society generally.

THE BAND OF HOPE

This Christian organisation have produced an excellent eight-page leaflet, 'Now You Know', which is a brief overview on drugs and costs 25p, or in wall-chart form costs £2.50. For more details contact The Band of Hope at 25f Copperfield Street, London SE1 0EN. Tel: 071-928 0848.

Drink BOOZE-UP lager because...

DRUGS

MEETING AIM
To provide accurate information about drugs, without getting into a lecture-mode. To share openly together opinions about drug use. To encourage your group to be honest about their views (eg many young people regard smoking cannabis as no worse than drinking alcohol, or smoking tobacco, even though it is still illegal). Also to examine the reasons why people take drugs and discover what the Bible says about the way we should treat our bodies.

M&M's
(15-20 mins)
Arrange for several bowls full of M&Ms to be in the room as your group arrive and invite them to take as many as they want with just one condition: they must only eat M&Ms of the same colour as the first one they choose (eg if the first sweet they eat is yellow, they can then only eat yellow M&Ms). Once everyone has arrived and eaten some M&Ms, explain the theme this week is drug abuse and that each M&M colour represented a different drug.

> Yellow = Cannabis
> Red = Ecstasy
> Brown = LSD
> Green = Anabolic steroids
> Orange = Solvents

Ask those who ate yellow M&Ms to describe as many different facts about cannabis that they can, eg street names, effects, dangers etc. List what they say on a whiteboard or OHP. Then fill in the blanks, and highlight any inaccuracies in their feedback without lecturing them. Make sure you get hold of a good up-to-date drug info booklet to base your comments on. Your GP or library should have some leaflets, or check out your local phone book for drug advice centres, or ring *Release* on 0171-729 9904 (Monday to Friday 10am 6pm) for drugs advice/info, or ring UK Band of Hope on 0171-928 0848 - for copies of their *Did You Know* support packs (£3.00).

They also hire out exhibition panels with drugs info.

WHAT THE USERS SAY
(15-20 mins)
Hand out pens and copies of the sheet opposite. Working in pairs ask the group to complete the sheets - allow about eight minutes for this. (NB You may prefer to read out the statements from the drug users.) Get the pairs to feedback to the main group

with their comments. In particular try to get the group to identify the main reasons why people take illegal drugs (eg to feel good, to escape reality, to get high/stoned, to relax, because everyone else does it, to temporarily change their personality).

WHAT'S WHAT
(5 mins)
Ask the group to say on a scale of 1 to 10 how available drugs are in their school/college (1 being not very available, 10 being easy to get hold of). Stress that you do not want names of people that deal/use drugs, merely an estimate of what drugs are sold and how available they are. Don't be too surprised if you get a wide range of answers to this question even from people in the same school/college. This is merely a rough and ready estimate to give you a feel for the scale and type of drug problem locally.

DRUGS DILEMMA
(10-15 mins)
In pairs ask the group to prepare a short role play on resisting the pressure to take drugs. The pairs can choose for themselves which drug the role play centres around. One person should adopt the role of a person who takes the drug and who wants his/her friend (the other person) to join them. The role play should focus around a conversation between the drug user who should use a range of gentle and then strong pressure tactics to get his/her friend to take the drug as well. Part of the persuasion could include phrases like; 'everyone's into this stuff,' or 'there's no real risk, it just makes you feel good,' etc.

The second person must try to resist the pressure to take the drug. What will they say in response to the persuasive pressure? Allow people a few minutes to prepare and rehearse and then everyone should perform their role play in front of the rest of the group. As these take place ask the group to comment and discuss the merits of the persuasive arguments taking place. In particular highlight any comments made by the person resisting the drugs which are particularly helpful for everyone to remember.

THE BIBLE & DRUGS
(10 mins)
Read the following verses and get the group in pairs or collectively, to write a one-sentence summary on the ways

they think each of the Scripture passages relate to the issue of drugs.

- 1 Corinthians 3:16-17
- 1 Corinthians 10:31
- Romans 12:1-2
- Galatians 6:7

Conclude by asking the group to summarise what you have talked about.

OPTIONAL EXTRAS

VIDEO
Show the first 14 minute section from the Edge 3 video on Addictive Behaviour. This excellent video is sure to promote lively discussion. Make sure you check out the helpful booklet which comes with the video which includes trigger questions and mini Bible studies on the subject. This video is available from local Christian bookstores or direct from Scripture Press (0494) 722151, £14.99.

DRUG TALK
Invite a speaker from a drug rehabilitation centre, a youth worker with experience of working with drug users/addicts, or a former user to come and talk to your group. The UK Band of Hope could provide a speaker and/or drug info resources. See the meeting plan on alcohol for their address. A quick-fire question and answer session may be a better alternative than a talk, unless you know the person is a very good speaker.

Beware: often former drug users tell stories of their former dependency and by doing this glamourise addiction. Ask any speakers to be careful not to do this.

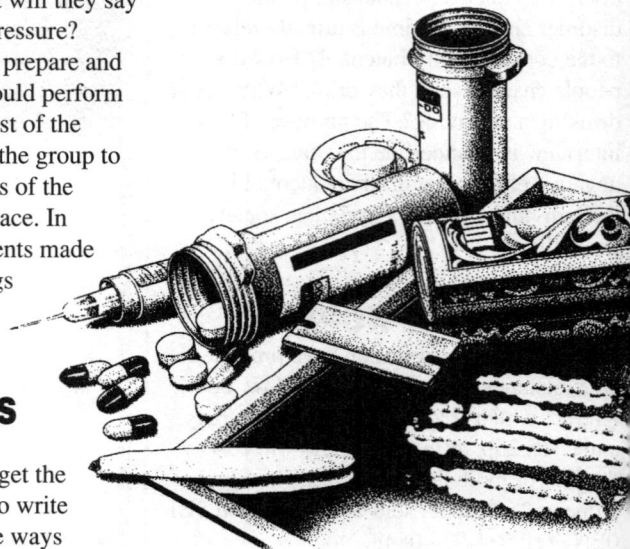

WHAT THE USERS SAY...

ECSTASY – CANNABIS – SOLVENTS –

Jay, 26

'The first E I had just blew my socks off completely... and then I got another one and it went on an on. Music enhances the drug. It was basically like unzipping the sound system and climbing in and being part of the music... People have said "You were trying to cope with problems in your life", but I didn't really have any problems - I just wanted to take the drugs, I enjoyed them.

I haven't done any Es since July 1992 when I got mixed up with an unpleasant dealer and had to get out of the area.

I went back to my mum's in Lincolnshire and had a kind of breakdown, seeing psychiatrists and things. Last time I worked was five years ago. I'd like to have a job but I'm getting anxiety attacks in supermarkets.

I reckon there were about 40 or 50 of us that went out every week and there's only two that have come through unharmed. Two have died, and loads ended up locked up for dealing or messed up with cabbage heads.'

Dale 16

'I love the kick you get from smoking puff. I take cannabis to get mildly stoned. There's no point in smoking so much you feel sick, I've done that a couple of times and it's stupid and besides I can't afford it. I smoke about an eighth [1/8th of an ounce] in three or four days. Usually I buy a bit more than I need and then sell it on at a profit to mates at school. I'm not really a dealer, but I wouldn't mind doing that, you can make quite a lot of money. I wouldn't deal in crack, that's stupid and you get put away for a long time if you get busted [caught by the police]. Some people say that smoking cannabis means you end up doing other drugs, but that ain't necessarily so. Trouble is, to get the stuff you have to go to some dodgy people, who might offer you an E, acid or a rock, that's when people get tempted. I've taken Es a couple of times, but I mainly stick to puff. My main ambition in life is to save up enough to buy a nine bar [9oz block of cannabis worth about £700].'

Eddie age 17

'I started taking gas when I was 14. Before then I tried thinners and glue once or twice. Until I took gas I was very quiet and kept to myself. After I had some friends, because the gas made me talk and open up. The day I started I was bored and I saw this can of lighter gas in my dad's house. I regret it now, but at the time it was OK. Your body soon gets used to it and soon it didn't have the same effect. After about a year I got depressed. I haven't taken any gas for nearly two years now. But before I could stop I got into serious trouble with the police twice and nearly got put away. I find it hard to make friends again, but I don't want to use gas to relax me.'

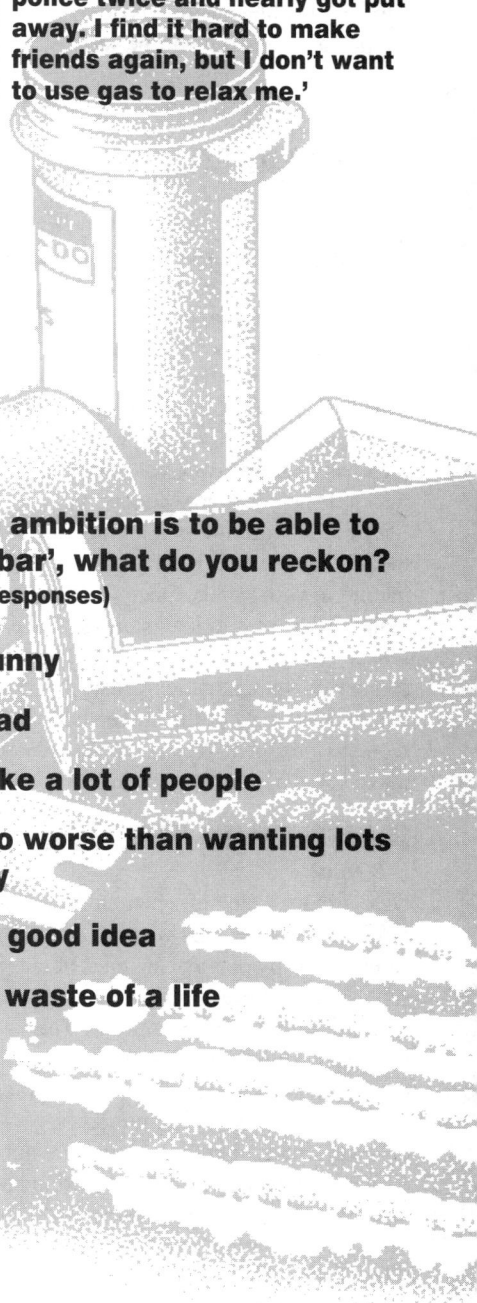

From the three statements above list some positive or enjoyable aspects of taking drugs.

....

....

....

....

....

From the statements above list some five negative or dangerous aspects of taking drugs.

....

....

....

....

....

Dale's main ambition is to be able to buy a 'nine bar', what do you reckon?
(tick up to two responses)

☐ That's funny

☐ That's sad

☐ That's like a lot of people

☐ That's no worse than wanting lots of money

☐ That's a good idea

☐ That's a waste of a life

NEW AGE

MEETING AIM
To examine some key beliefs of New Age and consider an appropriate Christian response.

PREPARATION
Preparing this session will involve some hard work! Sorry there's no short cut. You will have to read at least one good book about the New Age (eg Elliott Miller's *A Crash Course on the New Age Movement*, available from any Christian bookshop). You should also visit your local New Age shop or wholefood centre and pick up some magazines, such as *Kindred Spirit*, *Gaia* or *Resurgence*.

Inevitably, this meeting is quite a 'stationary' one. It won't be suitable for groups who need lots of physical activity or silly games to keep their interest up!

ICE BREAKER
(10 mins)
Tell the group a misleading story. Eg: a man is pushing a flashy sports car down the road. Eventually he pushes it up to a hotel, gives the hotel owner a lot of money, and leaves the car there He doesn't drive it away, nor does he actually enter the hotel. What on earth is he doing? Let the group ask you questions about it for a few minutes, until they realise the answer - or you tell them! - which is: he's playing Monopoly.

SAY: the reason it took a long time to get the answer was that you had the wrong picture in your minds. Once your picture of reality is sorted out, it all starts to make sense! Today we're looking at a 20th century movement which insists that our old, Bible-based view of the universe has to be radically changed. We need a new picture to make sense of reality.

IDENTIFYING THE NEW AGE
(15 min)
Give a short sketch of when the New Age movement started, and where it came from. Enliven this by playing snatches of current songs which express a New Age viewpoint - eg some stuff by The Shamen or The Levellers. Show the ying-yang symbol on the OHP, and discuss what other trappings have become popular (eg rainbows, crystals). Stress that these things are not wrong in themselves - but we need to be aware that they are also expressions of a powerful, persuasive movement

Test their awareness by dividing them into groups and giving them this true/false sheet to complete...

Some of these statements are TRUE and some are FALSE. Which is which?
● New Agers are all travellers and live in caravans. (False: many New Agers are most annoyed that the phrase 'New Age travellers' has become popular - most convoy dwellers are pretty ignorant about New Age ideas.)
● There are doctors and scientists in the New Age. (True: one of the first important books was *The Tao of Physics* by Austrian New Age scientist Fritjof Capra.)
● New Agers are hostile to Christianity. (False: they see it as just one of many spiritual options. Radical priests like Father Matthew Fox, and places such as the Centre for Creation Spirituality at St James', Piccadilly, have brought New Age thinking into Christian circles.)
● New Agers are behind the green movement. (True if you mean that they support it. False if you mean that it's a New Age conspiracy which Christians can safely ignore!)
● New Agers are interested in spiritual experiences. (True: they believe that by altering our state of consciousness, we become better, more fulfilled, more sensitive human beings, at one with the purposes of creation. So almost any spiritual route will do.)

Check the results and use each point as a way of giving a little more information.

NEW AGE BELIEFS #1
(5 mins)
Ask the group to name all the signs of the zodiac that they can remember - and then try to put them in order! After they have done their best, put the 'official' zodiac on the OHP, and say: the New Age Movement is based on the idea that each of these signs controls an 'age' in the world's history. The last 2000 years has been the age of Pisces, the fish sign - a very technological, industrial, analytical age, in which science and logic have flourished, men have dominated women, and Christianity has been the major religious force.

We are now moving into the age of Aquarius - the water bringer. Water is a symbol of spiritual power, which is now going to be sprinkled on the earth in many different forms. That's why there are so many different spiritual paths within the New Age movement (Show them a magazine such as *Kindred Spirit* and point out how many kinds of therapies, techniques and philosophies are mentioned). Christianity will survive, but only as one option in an era of universal peace and harmony, in which politics, education and personal relationships will be transformed, and human beings will recognise their spiritual relationship with the whole of creation.

NEW AGE BELIEFS #2
(10+ mins)
Divide them into small groups and hand out pens and a photocopy of the statement opposite on New Age views. What should Christians applaud in it? Where would they disagree?

CAN WE SAY?
(15 mins)
Analysing this statement may take a long time, for some groups, and may give you all that's needed to launch a discussion on how Christians can combat New Age ideas. But if not, it's vital that you spend some time before the end in helping people think about how to answer New Age claims. You could give each small group an area to work on:

● **CREATION** (Psalm 8)
● **HUMAN BEINGS** (Romans 3)
● **GOD** (Isaiah 40)
● **THE FUTURE** (2 Peter 3)

Ask them to prepare a report answering two questions:
(a) What's the difference between New Age and Christian teaching in this area?
(b) Why do you believe Christianity is right and the New Age is wrong?

SUMMARY
(5 min)
After each group has reported back, and the others have had a chance to criticise or learn from their results, sum up everything you have discussed in this meeting: what the New Age is, and how they will meet it; what it believes, and how it differs from Christianity; how we can answer its arguments. If some people want to keep thinking, offer a good Christian book that they can read on the subject.

Conclude by reading out Ephesians 6:12. Stress that New Agers are not 'the enemy'. We combat the evil, dangerous forces behind their ideas - but we love them and pray for them. End in prayer together.

We are all children of our mother, the Earth, and so we should be at one with each other. In each of us is the same divine spark. 'God' means different things to different people, but ultimately he, she or it is the power that runs through creation, shaping life and transforming it in the direction of harmony and unity. We need to take care of this planet - it's all we've got. We urgently need to develop our spiritual potential through all available means of heightening consciousness: meditation, magic, yoga, biofeedback - they are all routes to realizing our spiritual nature and our godlikeness. In the Aquarian Age, old forms of religious practice and new scientific discoveries about the brain will come together to enhance our ability to relate to 'God'. We must not be pessimistic about the future. Humanity will survive because it is part of a great cosmic evolutionary drive towards harmony and simplicity. We need to be people of truth and goodness, people with a respect for creation and for one another, in order to cooperate with the future. Let's not become enmeshed in personal guilt about our failings, but simply realize the divine power that dwells in us all.

What should Christians applaud in this statement?

....

....

....

....

On what points do Christians disagree with this statement?

....

....

....

....

SUPER HEROES

MEETING AIM

To consider some modern-day heroes and heroines and ask, 'What is a hero?' And to help the group realise that the Bible 'heroes' they read about were ordinary men and women who had flaws as well as good qualities.

LAST ACTION HERO
(15 mins)

Many people think the ultimate male hunk hero is Arnold Schwarznegger in his *Conan the Barbarian, Last Action Hero*-type films. Here is the chance to discover if there are any Arnie-like heroes in your youth group with this wild icebreaker game!

Ask for three of four male volunteers. Offer a good prize for the winner - something they will all want to win.

Prepare beforehand some questions - you'll need at least 15 easy questions and 15 tough questions. Explain to the volunteers that the winner is the first person to reach 100 points, or the person with the highest points after 10 minutes, whichever happens first. Points are won by correctly answering a question - 10 points for easy questions and 40 points for hard questions. However, if a contestant gets a hard question wrong they must complete a Arnie forfeit or lose 40 points!

Arnie forfeits could include: eating a large leaf of cooked cold cabbage, bursting a large inflated balloon with your teeth, swallowing the juice from a freshly squeezed lemon, eating the contents of a jar of baby food, putting your feet into wellies filled with cold custard etc!

WHAT MAKES A HERO?
(15 mins)

Hand out pen and paper and get the group to list 10 modern-day heroes or heroines and include their qualities, eg good actor, sexy body, compassionate, brave.

SAY: 'There is a world of difference between Mother Teresa and Robbie from Take That, and yet they are both modern-day heroes. So a wide variety of qualities and personalities can put a person onto the level of a hero or heroine.

Discuss:
● Can anyone become a hero or heroine?
● Name some heroes or heroines who have been manufactured by publicity and hype. What image has been created for that person? Do they really have any genuinely heroic qualities? If yes, what are they?
● Who is your hero or heroine and why?
● When is hero-worship unhealthy?

SPIRITUAL SUPER-HEROES
(20 mins)

The Bible seems chock-full of spiritual super-heroes. We think of these heroes and heroines as 'spiritual giants' but did they always get it right?

Hand out the sheet opposite, Bibles and pens, and ask people in small groups or as individuals to check out the Bible verses and fill in the blanks of the positive and negative actions of some spiritual super-heroes. Ask different people to start with different super-heroes, as there will not be enough time for all of them to complete all four sections.

Allow 15 minutes for this exercise and then get people to feed back their answers.

WRAP-UP TALK
(5 mins)

Explain that David blew it several times in his life, most notably when he committed adultery with Bathsheba and then arranged the death of her husband. However, when he was found out he didn't try to blame others or justify his actions, he took the blame and admitted he had sinned.

Tell people to check out Psalm 51 if they want to discover how David said sorry to God and repented.

Conclude by challenging the group to choose their heroes and heroines carefully. Many of our heroes or screen idols do not have a life worth copying. St Paul told people to 'imitate me as I imitate Christ' (Phillipians 3:17). Although we may think we are nobodies, as we follow Christ and his example we can do heroic deeds. Even making a major mistake (and you can't do much worse than David) doesn't necessarily mean we can't be a hero or heroine in God's eyes.

MIXED UP HEROES
(10 mins)

Can you identify the mixed-up personalities in the picture? The answers are at the bottom of the page.

Look through some magazines (*TV Hits, Smash Hits* etc) and cut out photographs of famous personalities, pop stars etc, to make this fun intro game on the subject of heroes and heroines.

You will need at least 20 photographs. Then cut horizontally through the pictures and match two different pictures together. Label them 1a, 1b, 2a, 2b, etc.

Prior to the start of the meeting, blue-tack the mixed-up photos around the room where your youth group meet.

As the youngsters arrive, give each paper and a pen and ask them to list as many of the personalities as possible.

Play some suitable background music during the game eg 'I need a hero' by Tina Turner.

OPTIONAL EXTRAS

Ask the group to find out who their parent(s')/guardians' heroes or heroines were during their teenage years, and why. Report back and share findings next week.

ANSWER

Top: Joey Lawrence, *Bottom:* Pamela Anderson.

SUPER-HEROES	ACTIONS OF SUPER-HEROES	
	Positive Actions	Negative Actions
ABRAHAM **Genesis 12:1-20;** **14:17-22;** **15:1-6;** **16:1-6;** **22:17-18.**		
MOSES **Exodus 2:11-12;** **chaps 3-6;** **12:37;** **14:21-29.**		
DAVID **1 Samuel 16:1-13;** **chap 17;** **24:10-12;** **2 Samuel chaps** **8, 11 & 12.**		
PETER **Matthew 14:22-33;** **16:13-17;** **26:69-75.**		

Book Four:
Belief

'**D**octrine-zzz' is how most young people regard the subject which these meetings cover. John Allan and I hope that the plans we have written will help you to bring to life these vital doctrinal strands of the Christian faith.

Is Christianity true? Did Jesus really come back to life? Is Jesus returning to earth? And if so when and why? These are just some of the vital questions we want young people to wrestle with and we believe these meeting plans can help you facilitate that investigation.

READY-TO-USE-MEETING GUIDE

PUBLICITY PAGE

Get your meeting noticed by using the ready-to-photocopy artwork below to promote the series/first meetings. Simply add the details of venue and time and photocopy onto paper or card for an eye-catching poster. This image can also be shrunk to use as a personal invite.

WHAT IS DOCTRINE?

MEETING AIM:

To introduce the theme of doctrine – explain what doctrine is and show how it can protect us from being taken in by a cult or some crazy new teaching.

BROOM BALANCE (5 mins)

Apply three metres of masking tape in a straight line across the floor/carpet and hold up a £10 note. Tell your group that you want three volunteers to attempt to walk from one end of the tape to the other in a straight line, and whoever can do it gets the £10 note!

Before their 'turn' each person must hold a broomstick at arm's length above their heads and look at the tip of the boom while you spin them around 10 times. Get the group to count with you as you turn them round. Then quickly take the broom away, position them at the start of the line and give them 10 seconds to walk straight along the tape.

It's important to keep the area clear of chairs, tables, etc, and to be ready to catch them as they stagger and fall through dizziness. If you ensure the volunteers keep their eyes open and fixed on the tip of the broom while you quickly turn them round ten times your £10 should be safe!

WALK STRAIGHT (10 mins)

Read out Ephesians 4:11-16 then re-read verse 13 and 14.

Briefly explain that the game illustrates what Paul meant when he wrote to the church in Ephesus that they should not get 'blown about by every shifting wind of teaching'. The way to avoid getting dizzy and easily tricked into believing any old thing is to become 'mature' Christians, that is people who know a bit more than the very basics of Christianity and who put this deeper knowledge and experience about God into practice in their lives.

This series of meetings aims to explain what the core truths of Christian teaching (doctrine) are so that we can better avoid getting 'blown about'.

Make the point that since the beginning of the church nearly 2,000 years ago lots of different people and groups have tried to add to or change the basic beliefs of Christianity. Sometimes a lot of people have left the mainstream church to join a new group who claim some new or secret teaching.

The early church decided on a statement which listed what the central beliefs of Christianity were. Since the first statement or 'creed' was made, called the Apostles Creed, several others were written to counter heresies. For example the Nicene Creed adopted by the church 300 years after the death of Christ was formulated to counter a heresy that denied that Jesus really was the divine Son of God. About 50 years later another creed called the Athanasian Creed was agreed on which emphasised the Trinity of God and that Jesus was really born as a baby. Again this was to counter the views of splinter groups from the church who had left the central truths.

The word 'creed' comes from the Latin word *credo* which means 'I believe'.

Although there is no full-scale creed in the New Testament, credal statements exist which later Christians built upon; eg, Ephesians 4:5; Philippians 2:16.

Conclude this section by explaining that later you'll look together at one of the earliest creeds the church formulated. But first...

MIX AND MATCH (5-10 mins)

Hand out copies of the quizsheet opposite plus a pencil or pen. Read out the instructions at the top of the sheet and give people a few minutes to complete it. Then read out the answers (below).

SAY: Because doctrine is often connected with posh or complicated sounding words it is easy to get put off and think that doctrine is only important for biblical scholars and theological academics. The truth is that doctrine is important to us all because it is about the key principles (plus the not-so-central ones) which we believe. So we shouldn't get bothered by the long words, just concentrate on what they mean!

ANSWERS: 1f; 2d; 3c; 4e; 5a; 6g; 7b.

I BELIEVE... (15 mins)

As individuals ask your youngsters to write their own creed (on the bottom half of their quizsheet). This should be a brief personal statement of what they believe about God the Father, Son and Holy Spirit, the church and what they believe a Christian is.

Encourage them to personalise their 'I believe...' by including details of what they think the character of God is like and how the church and Christians should be. Stress that you are not looking for the most 'correct' version but a creed which illustrates what they believe now. Therefore they are allowed to include their doubts about God, because you want them to say what they *actually* believe, not what they think they *should* believe.

Allow people up to 10 minutes to write it down. Play some soft background music while they work. Then either collect the creeds and read them out, or if the group are confident, ask them to read their creeds out to everyone else.

If your group are honest and open, you will find this exercise to be a helpful way of gauging exactly what the members of your group believe - or not as the case may be. It could be an eye-opener!

THE APOSTLES CREED

I believe in God, the Father almighty,
creator of heaven and earth.
I believe in Jesus Christ, his only Son, our Lord.
He was conceived by the power of the Holy Spirit and born of the Virgin Mary,
He suffered under Pontius Pilate,
was crucified, died, and was buried.
On the third day he rose again.
He ascended into heaven,
and is seated at the right hand of the Father.
He will come again to judge the living and the dead.
I believe in the Holy Spirit,
the holy catholic Church,
the communion of the saints,
the forgiveness of sins,
the resurrection of the body,
and the life everlasting.

THE APOSTLES CREED (10-15 mins)

Depending on your group, you could make this next section an act of liturgical worship, a comparison exercise with what they wrote for their creed, or both.

Explain that this well-known creed was not actually written by one of the first apostles (disciples), although it is named after them. It was written after the last book in the New Testament was written, but has always held an important place in the church. This creed has often been used by mainstream branches of the Christian church through the centuries as a test of faith.

WE BELIEVE... (5 mins)

Conclude by reading your own church's 'Statement or Articles of Faith' (if there is one) and/or by together saying or singing 'We Believe' (by Graham Kendrick).

End by praying that God will reveal truth during the series coming up and so help every member of the group to understand and love him better.

MIX & MATCH

Doctrines are important principles which together form a whole system of belief. So the Christian doctrines together make up the Christian faith. 'Doctrine' may seem like a dry and unimportant word, but over the centuries many Christians have suffered and died to help keep the core doctrines (beliefs) about the Christian faith intact.

A range of different doctrines are listed below left. See if you can match up the doctrines with the correct definition on the right by drawing a line between them. For example, if you think pneumotology is the doctrine about the birth of Christ then draw a line between (1) and (a).

Although many of the words seem long and complicated several hold clues to their meaning. The first part of the word Pneumotology sounds like pneumatic (as in pneumatic tyre - a tyre inflated by air) this may give a clue as to its meaning.

DOCTRINE	DEFINITION
1) pneumotology	a) beliefs about the birth of Christ
2) baptism	b) beliefs about angels
3) eschatology	c) beliefs about the last days
4) ecclesiology	d) beliefs about initiation into the church
5) incarnation	e) beliefs about the church
6) soteriology	f) beliefs about the Holy Spirit
7) angelology	g) beliefs about salvation

Personal Creed

Name..

Date..

I believe ....

....

....

....

....

....

....

....

....

....

....

....

THE TRUTH

MEETING AIM:

To show that humankind's eternal search for ultimate truth is an important one. To help young people begin to grapple with fundamental philosophical questions and encourage them to keep asking, searching, and exploring for truth.

TELLING THE TRUTH
(10 mins)

Pre-arrange with two of your group for them to take part in this experiment. Explain to the rest of the group that two volunteers are each going to give two accounts of what they did yesterday. One account will be truthful, the other will be a lie. (Alternatively they could give two accounts of anything else, so long as one is truthful, one a lie).

Explain to the volunteers that you want them to try and make the false story just as convincing as the truthful one.

The volunteers should take up to two minutes on each story and allow the group up to four questions which the volunteer should answer. It is important that they provide totally truthful replies to the truthful account, but they can tell any amount of fibs about the false story.

The group have to determine which two of the four accounts were truthful. However, half of the youngsters trying to discover the truth should be blindfolded while the two volunteers give their stories. This means these can only listen to the stories, while the rest have the benefit of listening and observing.

Before the experiment begins ask everyone: 'Will the blindfolded listeners/questioners do as well as the unblindfolded ones in determining which of the stories are truthful?'

After they make their decision, begin the experiment. Then ask the listening/questioning groups to vote for which two accounts were truthful. Keep a score on whether the blindfolded or unblindfolded groups did best.

Conclude by revealing which stories were truthful and tell them that blind people are not allowed to sit on juries because they cannot observe the witnesses making their statements or being cross-examined. Most people think that body language helps give away someone who is lying. However, experiments have proved that the opposite is true and that by just focusing on what people say we can better choose the truth. This is because people tend to talk too much, leave odd pauses, or make some other unusual verbal blunder when they lie, whereas most adults can control their body language when lying.

TRUTH BUSTERS
(15 mins)

You will need a large pile of recent newspapers for this next exercise, plus scissors, glue, felt-tipped pens and large A2 pieces of card.

Divide the youngsters into groups of three of four and give each small group a pile of papers. Their task is to sift through the papers and cut out the stories which relate to the issue of 'truth' (eg, court cases where the truth is trying to be discovered; a married man or woman accused of lying by their partner in a divorce case; people like politicians accused of lying).

Then ask the small groups to paste their stories onto the card and add their own questions and comments (eg, O.J. Simpson is innocent'. Question to John Major: 'Do you know more about selling guns to Iraq than you're letting on?')

Allow up to twelve minutes for this exercise and then pin the cards on the wall and invite reaction and comments to each group's work.

End this section by asking: 'What would the world be like if everyone told the truth and knew the truth about everything?'

TRUE OR FALSE
(8 mins)

Hand out copies of the worksheet to each individual and ask them to decide which statements are true, and which are false.

Allow up to five minutes for them to decide on the answers, and then read them out. Apart from being fun, this exercise shows that some facts do not neatly fit the true or false box since they cannot be proved to be true or false. For these questions (No. 5, 9, 10, 14), individuals get a mark for a correct answer whether they marked 'true' or 'false' as the answer. Come back to this point when you discuss questions 2) and 6) in the 'What is Truth' section.

ANSWERS

1) False (Yorkshire), 2) True, 3) True, 4) False (their health), 6) True, 7) False (golf), 8) False (sheep), 11) False (sulphuric), 12) True, 13) True, 15) False (Sudan), 16) False (Pele), 17) True, 18) True, 19) False (Philippines), 20) True.

WHAT IS TRUTH?
(20 mins)

Discuss this statement:-

'Is the truth restricted only to those things we can prove are true?' (For example, in a court case hearsay evidence is not admissible; the judge requires evidence - that is, facts that can be proved to be true.)

This is the backbone of this meeting plan so read this section through carefully before the meeting and think about how you will encourage all the members in your group to take part in discussing these issues.

Encourage the group to explore these arguments:

1) If a fact cannot be proved to be true, it is just an opinion that one person holds.

2) If a fact is true, it remains true even if it cannot be proved. (For example, if Darren kills Rachel, the truth is he is a murderer, even if there is no evidence to incriminate him.)

3) A person can sincerely believe that they know the truth about something, but they can be sincerely wrong or even deluded.

4) Two people can see the same event or incident and yet give widely differing accounts. Their perception of the truth differs because of their proximity to the event, their background, their sympathies for one 'side', their state of mind at the time, and lots of other factors.

5) People can be indoctrinated by propaganda so much that they will sincerely believe anything they are told - even the most stupid and obvious lie.

6) Going back to the murder of Rachel by Darren - the weakness of the human ability to determine the truth of an incident does not affect the basic facts. We may be unable to determine the truth, but the fact remains that it was Darren who killed Rachel. The 'truth' may be undiscovered, but it remains so.

7) One group of ancient Greek philosophers we called 'sophists' believed that humans cannot know the answers to important philosophical questions like 'Is there a God?' In philosophy this view is called 'scepticism'. Do you think most people today are sceptics? What are the dangers of being sceptical about important issues?

8) Why do people always seem to want these ultimate truths answered? (People need absolutes - they give boundaries, context, a framework, guidance and structure - the alternative is anarchy.)

LIAR, LUNATIC OR LORD?
(15 mins)

SAY: 'Probably the most important doctrine (belief) about God is that God exists. If there is no God, there is no Christianity.

'Built on this crucial belief is the doctrine that God is true. If God is not true to his own words, if he is unable to decide what is truth, if his knowledge is limited and fallible, then again, the whole Christian faith crumbles into a heap.

'Built on the foundation that God exists and he is true, is a third fundamental basic belief which says that the Bible is God's word and is a truthful record of the way God deals with people.

'Believing in God doesn't mean kissing goodbye to your brains, or pretending that it doesn't matter if God isn't real and true.

'St Paul taught that if the basics of the Christian faith are not true our faith is futile and we should be pitied for wasting our lives. However, he was so convinced of the truth of the message that he was prepared to endure various sufferings and ultimately death.

'Jesus claimed to be the Son of God and the source of truth. This means either he was a liar - telling untruths, or he was deluded - a lunatic, or his words were true, and he was who he claimed - the Lord.'

Challenge your group to decide which one they think is true: Liar, Lunatic or Lord.

Then say:

'Over half of the New Testament's references to truth appear in John's writings. John records Jesus saying that true disciples must continue in his words - and in that way will 'know the truth and the truth will set them free' (John 8:31,32).'

Ask your group to check out the following verses in John's Gospel and write down in their own words what these scriptures say about 'truth'.

● John 8:31,32 ● John 14:6 ● John 16:3
● John 17:3 ● John 18:37 ● John 8:4

Get some feedback and then read out or put onto an OHP these quotes:

'The object of philosophy, as I conceive it, is not to help people, but to discover truth.'
(C.E.M. Joad, English philosopher, 1891-1953)

'Truth is reality revealed. Jesus is the truth because in him the sum of the qualities hidden in God is presented and revealed to the world.' (A.H. Strong *Systematic Theology* p261)

'Everyone who cares for truth, who has any feeling for the truth, recognises my voice.'
(Jesus - recorded in John 18:37, *The Message*)

Close by briefly praying to God, inviting him to reveal is his truth to all the group through the Holy Spirit. Then allow for a period of quiet, or play a worship song.

TRUE OR FALSE

True False

1) The white rose is the symbol of Lancashire.

2) There are 500 centimetres in five metres.

3) William Kellogg first manufactured Corn Flakes in 1906.

4) Hypochondriac's worry about open spaces.

5) There is life on other planets somewhere in outer space.

6) Aluminium is made from bauxite.

7) A spoon, a brassie, and a niblick are all used in connection with croquet.

8) A 'merino' is a type of goat.

9) Glasgow Rangers play the most attractive football of any club side in Europe.

10) God always has and always will exist.

11) Lactic acid is used in car batteries.

12) The elephant is a national emblem of India.

13) A narcotic drug induces sleep.

14) Men are better at telling jokes than women.

15) Egypt is the largest country (by land area) in Africa.

16) The soccer star, Edson Arantes do Nascimento is better known as Maradona.

17) The first woman to fly from Britain to Australia was Amy Johnson.

18) If you add together the number of gospels, with the number of commandments and multiply the figure by the number of testaments the total is 28.

19) After the assassination of her husband, Cory Aquino became a political leader in Columbia.

20) Europe has a longer coastline than Africa.

THE BILL

MEETING AIM:
To show that God gave us commands not to spoil our lives, but because guidelines are the best way for us to live our lives to the full.

ON THE BEAT
(10 mins)
Show a videoed clip from a TV police-drama. Choose a clip that shows someone getting chased and caught by the police.

Ask your group to write down a question they would like to ask a real police officer. It could be about their reasons for being a copper, the most difficult arrest they ever made, or something more controversial, such as, why do police seem to pick on young people who hang around on the streets? Or, should all police officers be armed?

Collect in the questions and then explain that later that evening a police officer will be dropping in to answer their questions.

If there isn't a member of the police service that attends your church ask around some other churches. Alternatively you could contact the Christian Police Association (0116-2412416) who may be able to recommend a suitable person.

LEGAL EAGLES
(5 mins)
Test people's legal knowledge by asking which of the following is a criminal offence:
1) Trespassing on someone else's land.
2) Glue sniffing.
3) An Australian who arrived in the UK yesterday is caught committing a minor criminal offence but excuses himself because he was ignorant of British law.
4) Obstructing a vicar and stopping him from giving a sermon at a church service.
5) Threatening to damage someone's property.

ANSWERS:
1 and 2 are not criminal offences; the rest are.
3) Ignorance is not a defence. 4) This breaks the Offences Against the Persons Act 1861, with a penalty of up to two years imprisonment!

ANARCHY RULES OK?
(10 mins)
Play a popular game that the group enjoys. Choose one with plenty of fixed rules where you usually act as the referee, eg five-a-side or unihock.

Without telling them, fail to penalise any rule breaking, fouls etc. It will usually take a group about three to five minutes to realise

what is going on - and then you need to choose carefully when to intervene!

Let the game run on long enough for tempers to get frayed, disputes argued over and the game to be spoiled.

Stop the game and ask the group for their reactions to the situation.

ASK:
Why wasn't it much fun? Was it fun for some and not for others? Why? Why do we need rules and a referee to enforce them? What would be the consequence if our society had no rules and no law enforcers?

WISHFUL THINKING
(10 mins)
Hand out photocopies of the 'Wishful Thinking' worksheet and pens and ask everyone to imagine they have the power to change, abolish or invent some new laws. What would they do? Allow a couple of minutes thinking and writing time, then ask them to share their ideas. Get the group to vote on the most popular law change. Alternatively, if you have a large group, you could get them to vote for a new 10 Commandments.

Get a group member to read out Exodus 20:1-17. Ask the group, how would things be different if:
● everyone kept the 10 Commandments?
● the 10 Commandments were called the 10 Suggestions?

KEEP TAKING THE TABLETS
(5 mins)
SAY:
The 10 Commandments were written by God himself onto stone tablets. These stone blocks were treated by the Jews as very important. They were placed inside the most valuable piece of furniture the nation owned - the ark of the covenant. But why were these stone tablets so valuable? It was because they were written by God himself and because they represented a covenant - a promise, a contract between God and the people. (Read out Exodus 19:5).

We don't use stone tablets today, but we do have documents that contain covenants, promises or legal contracts, and these are treated as very important pieces of paper. What documents can you think of? (Deeds of a house, marriage and birth certificates, Magna Carta, etc.)

God set out a way of living and promised

THE BILL © THAMES TELEVISION

that those who kept to his way would be fulfilled. Jesus underlined this himself when he said, 'I have come to give you life to the full' (John 10:10).

The bad news is we have all broken God's laws (Romans 3:23), but the good news is if we are truly sorry we can be forgiven by God (1 John 1:9) - and this is a promise - from God!

Breaking the rules always has a consequence: innocent people can get hurt; you could get hurt; you could be punished. The Bible teaches that the result of breaking God's rules is death - eternal separation from God. We can pay the penalty ourselves or let Jesus. The choice is ours!

MEET THE BILL
(20 mins)
Some young people are hostile towards the police. Think carefully before simply going ahead with this part of the meeting plan. With a suitable police officer, however, who can relate easily to teenagers and who is preferably him/herself a Christian, it can start a helpful and lively debate.

OPTIONAL EXTRAS

COVENANT MAKERS
Hand out photocopied sheets of the Covenant Makers worksheet and pens and ask the group to write out a kind of 'covenant' between themselves and God. It is up to them what it says. It could include a Bible verse which is itself a promise or contract, eg Proverbs 3:5-6.

Then arrange to meet one or two of your group at a Burger Bar sometime in the next week for a Big Mac, a coke and a chat. Ask them to bring along the covenant sheet they wrote up and explain you would like to talk with them about where they are with God. Pray for a significant time!

WISHFUL THINKING

Imagine you have the power to change, abolish or invent a law. What would it be? Write it down in the space provided and then write down what you consider will be the advantages and disadvantages of your altered, abolished or new law.

....

....

....

....

Advantages...

....

....

Disadvantages..

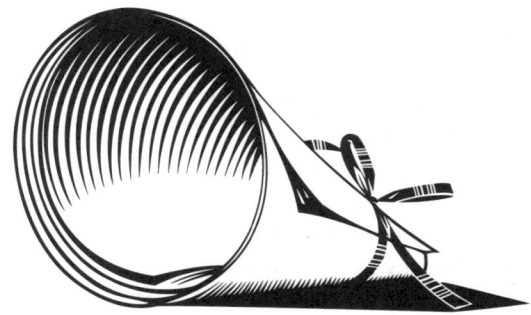

....

....

A Covenant between me and God

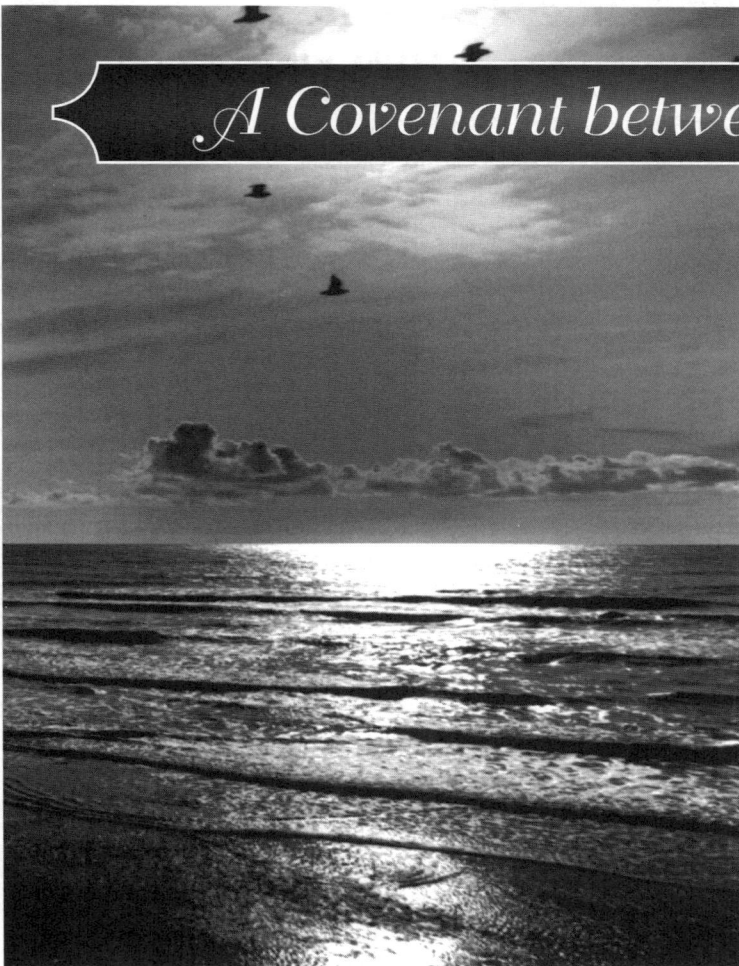

....

....

....

....

....

....

....

....

....

....

....

....

Signed ....

Date ....

THE ATONEMENT

MEETING AIM:
To give group members a clear understanding of the meaning of Jesus' death, and its central importance to Christian faith.

PREPARATION
Photocopy the image (far right) onto paper or thin card (one per small group). Then cut along the lines.

Find two large safety pins and practise the trick outlined below. Get hold of a metal tray, sheets of paper, lighter fluid and a *heatproof surface* for the final item. Read some background material - for example, chapters 14,15 and 18 of James Packer's book *Knowing God,* Hodders).

MAKING IT ONE
(10 mins)
Divide into small groups. Give each group a copy of the cut-up square, and see who can re-assemble it first, using all the pieces and making an exact square. When one group has won, explain that this introduces tonight's subject: how God takes people who were fragmented by divisions and far away from him, and brings them together in himself. Read out Ephesians 2:13-18.

The word 'atonement' was invented in mediaeval days because there wasn't really such a word in English. It's about how we become 'at one' with God. What's the central shape in the square? The cross. The Ephesians passage stresses that the cross is the centre of atonement.

NOBODY'S PERFECT
(15 mins)
Why do we need atonement? Because nobody is good enough to please God by his or her own efforts. This leaves God with a problem: his *justice* means that he can't just ignore evil, but his *love* means that he wants to forgive us.

Divide the group into two, and play a short game of basketball, football, or anything else that requires a referee. At first play it by the rules. After a few minutes, two of the players (whom you have previously 'planted') begin to play unfairly and commit obvious fouls. Ignore this for as long as you can, and then when the protests begin to rise, blow the whistle. But instead of awarding a penalty, say, 'I think we'll forget that one, but don't do it again,' and restart play with a throw-in. Keep going until they are nearly ready to lynch you...

Explain to the group: justice demands

In July 1978, 48-year-old Bill Quinlan and his 18-year-old nephew David Lucas set sail from San Diego on a 4000-mile voyage to the Galapagos Islands. After 1,000 miles, their trimaran was smashed by a hurricane. They drifted for five days on their life-raft, until only one can of water and two cans of food were left. Then Quinlan suddenly said to Lucas: 'You are only 18. You have a full life ahead of you.' He jumped into the water, evading Lucas' attempts to stop him, and started to swim away.

Lucas was rescued. And he gave Quinlan's wife, Vicki, the two mementos his uncle had left, a gold ring and a tin on which he had scratched the words 'I love you. I'm sorry'.

Bill Quinlan gave his life so that somebody else could live. Sound familiar?

even, fair treatment. If rules are broken, punishment needs to follow. Love and justice belong together. This is why God can't just ignore sin. It matters to him much more than it matters to us. And his love for us led him to bring about the plan of atonement.

PICTURES
(10 mins)
In small groups, look at these verses: 1 Timothy 2:5-6; Colossians 1:21-22; Hebrews 9:27-28. Then in 'Pictionary' style, draw some pictures on the OHP and ask the group to guess which words from the verses are being referred to: a bag of money being handed over at gunpoint (ransom); someone standing in the middle between two other people (mediator - you may need to give some clues with this one); two people embracing (reconciliation); an animal on an altar (sacrifice).

Tell them that these are four of the main pictures the New Testament uses to illustrate what Jesus did by dying for us: he paid a price to set us free; he brought two sides together; he made peace between God and human beings; and he offered himself as a sacrifice. Take time to explain these concepts carefully, perhaps illustrating with a story such as that of Bill Quinlan.

WHAT KIND OF GOD...?
(10 mins)
Now put on the OHP (or circulate copies of) this statement:

'This idea about Christ sacrificing himself for us is horrible. What kind of a God would feel so bad-tempered about us that he would order his only son to die a horrible death to satisfy his blood lust? Anyway, I don't want anybody to pay for my sins, thank you very much. That's a cop-out. I'd rather be responsible for my own misdeeds.'

Get the group to discuss this objection together. What answer should Christians give? Then sum up the discussion, including these points:
(1) When the Bible talks about God's 'wrath', it doesn't mean bad temper. God doesn't lose control. God's wrath is his hatred of everything evil - and it's a good thing he does feel this way. We wouldn't want him to be complacent about Hitler, uncaring about Idi Amin, neutral about Rwanda.
(2) It isn't that God ordered an innocent third party to suffer for us in Jesus, God *himself* paid the penalty - he was both our judge and our substitute.
(3) It sounds noble and courageous to say 'I'll be responsible for myself,' but none of

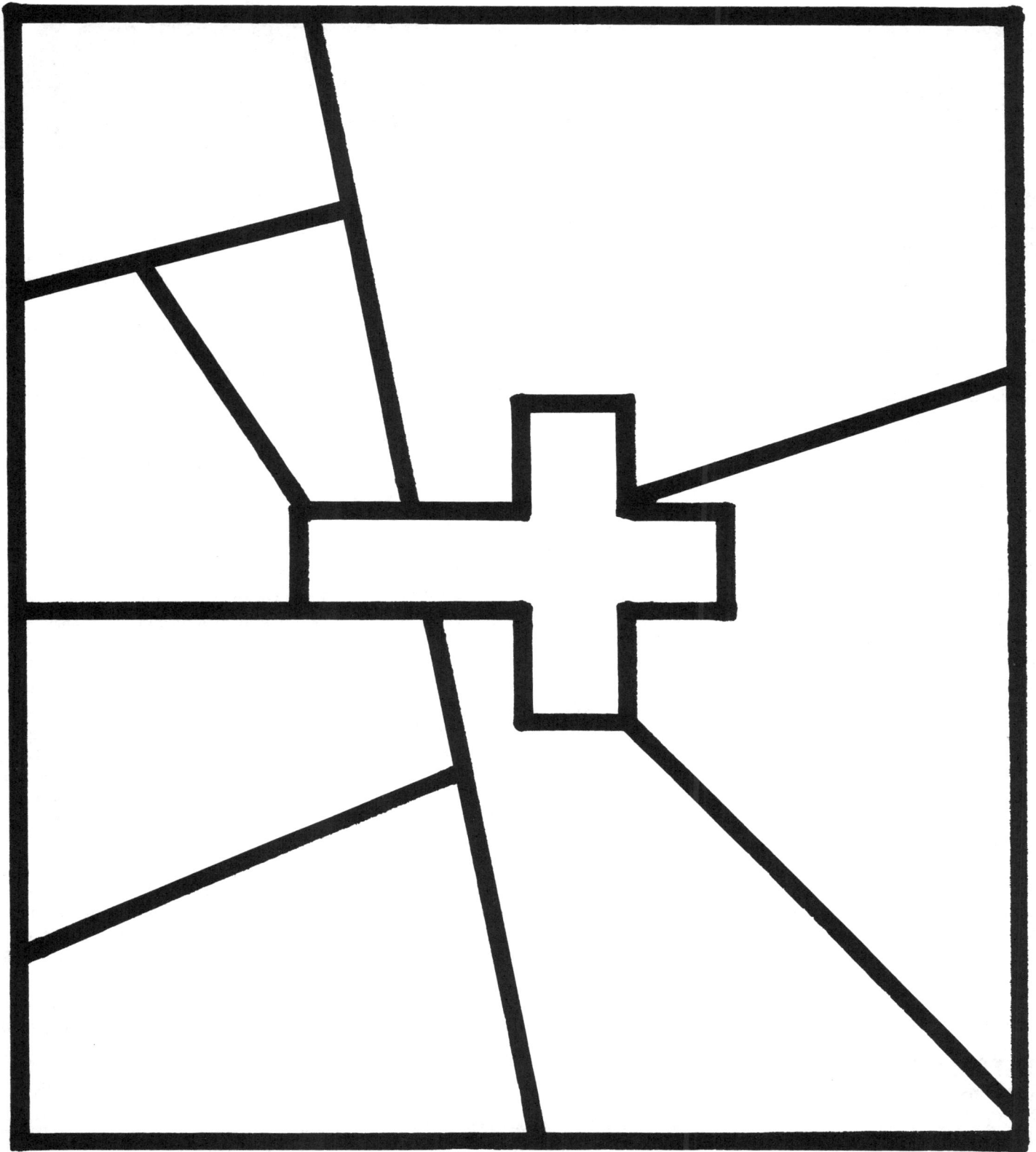

us can. We cannot make ourselves fit for God's presence; nor can we pay the price of our sins and win our own release. Without Jesus we have no hope.

THE SACRIFICE
(15 mins)

The way you do this will depend on the make-up of your group. Don't treat it too casually, but on the other hand don't let it lapse into sentimentality. Done properly, it can be a powerful visual demonstration of all you have been talking about.

Give each person a piece of paper and a pen. Ask them to write three things on the paper - stressing heavily that no one else will read this, not even you! **First:** the worst sin they think they have ever committed. **Second:** the most recent sin they can remember committing. **Third:** the most commonly repeated sin in their lives. Get them to fold up the paper securely, and heap the slips in a metal baking tray.

Carefully pour lighter fluid over all the slips. Read slowly Hebrews 9:26b: 'Christ has appeared once for all at the end of the ages to do away with sin by the sacrifice of himself' - and simultaneously toss a lighted match into the metal tray. There will be a spurt of flame, and the slips will be destroyed.

NB Take very great care not to pour too much lighter fuel onto the slips and ensure that everyone stands back from the tray.

Pray together, thanking God for the forgiveness of sin, and new life which is available in Jesus. If it's appropriate for your group, sing a song such as 'Such Love' while you watch the flames die down and disappear.

THE RESURRECTION

MEETING AIM:

To explore the credibility of the claim that Jesus rose from the dead, and then to ask: What does it mean? Why do Christians get so excited about the doctrine of the resurrection?

PREPARATION

As well as this outline, you will need a book which contains some of the basic evidence for the resurrection (eg, Josh McDowell's, *Evidence That Demands A Verdict* or *You Must Be Joking* by Michael Green). To construct the clues for the 'assault course' you will need to have a good grasp of some of the main points.

SHAKY FOUNDATIONS
(10 mins)

Divide into four small groups and issue each mini-group with three (blown up) balloons, a sheet of cardboard and a pack of cards (or, if you prefer, a bag of marshmallows). Their task is to place the cardboard on top of the balloons, and then - using the cardboard as a table - to build a card house using at least 20 cards (or build a stack of ten marshmallows, one on top of the other) without it all falling down.

Make the point that unless you're building on something rock-solid, crashes and disasters are likely to happen again and again. Now if the resurrection of Jesus Christ is a shaky foundation, Christians are in real trouble - because that's the base on which everything else depends.

Read the group 1 Corinthians 15:13-19 and pause to let it sink in.

ESTABLISHING THE FACTS
(30 mins)

So how far can we trust the Bible's claim? This section of the meeting is designed as a kind of assault course. It looks at the evidence against four big arguments: 'Jesus never died.' 'The disciples probably went to the wrong tomb.' 'The body was stolen.' 'The Jews or the Romans had the body all the time - they had just removed it somewhere else.' Make sure the group understand these arguments before you begin.

Get hold of one of those briefcases with a four-figure number lock. Put a box of chocolates inside it, close it and spin the dials. Show it to the group, and say that the first group to work out the combination and get into the case will be entitled to keep the

contents.

There are four stages to the 'assault course', each of which yields one of the numbers. Start different mini-groups at different stages, and let them go round each in turn, racing the others to crack the clues and learn the numbers.

For the first number, they have to listen to a short cassette tape on which you have pre-recorded a number of facts about the resurrection (leave a space between them in case they want to rewind and listen to one or two of them again).

Some of these facts help to disprove the theory that 'Jesus never died' (eg the blood and water that came from Jesus' side, the weight of the bandages, the impossibility of his shattered hands and feet pushing aside the stone and walking back into town). The rest of the facts will be quite irrelevant (eg 'The resurrection is mentioned in 1 Thessalonians 1:10', or 'Jesus died at the Passover weekend'). Their task is to count the relevant facts; make sure that the correct number is the same as the first digit in your combination lock!

For the second number, they have to tour the building looking for posters which read like this:

EVEN IF THE DISCIPLES HAD GONE TO THE WRONG TOMB, IT WOULD HAVE BEEN EASY FOR THE AUTHORITIES TO POINT OUT THE RIGHT ONE
75398.

Some of these posters will contain good arguments against the theory that 'the disciples went to the wrong tomb by mistake'. Others will contain bad or irrelevant arguments. All of the posters will have a group of numbers at the bottom, as above. When the group has sorted out the *good* ones from the *bad* ones, they will find that all the good ones contain one number in common. That number will give them the second digit.

For the third number, give out six cards bearing the following messages:

❶ Grave-robbers in those days weren't interested in bodies, but in the spices and jewels which were left with them. In Jesus' case, the body disappeared, but the spices were left. If this is TRUE, go to 3. If this is FALSE, go to 5. If this is THE END, your number is 5.

❷ The disciples were fanatically devoted to

Jesus and would not have let him disappear without a struggle. Therefore they could well have hatched a plot to fake his resurrection. If this is TRUE, go to 5. If this is FALSE, go to 6. If this is THE END, your number is 4.

❸ Jesus' body was wrapped up in bandages that would have taken some time to remove. Anyone stealing the body in a hurry would have taken the bandages as well as the body. And that's what happened. If this is TRUE, go to 2. If this is FALSE, go to 5. If this is THE END, your number is 2.

❹ The tomb of Jesus was sealed by the soldiers. It would have been treason against the Empire, punishable by instant death, to have broken the seal. If this is TRUE, go to 2. If this is FALSE, go to 5. If this is THE END, your number is 1.

❺ The soldiers were probably Roman troops who were always on the look-out for ways of making money. They could easily have been bribed by Jesus' sympathisers. If this is TRUE, go to 6. If this is FALSE, go to 4. If this is THE END, your number is 3.

❻ To carry the stolen body back into the city meant going past lots of houses where at this hot time of year, many people slept outside. And it was the one weekend when Jews weren't supposed to touch a dead body. If this is TRUE, go to 4, if this is FALSE, go to 1. If this is THE END, your number is... (Add the correct digit which they're looking for to the end of card 6.)

What the group must do is to arrange these cards in a straight line in the correct order. When they reach the final card (it's number 6) they will be able to read the missing digit.

For the fourth number, they have to read Acts 4:1-4, 13-21, and then give you three good reasons why it's impossible to say, 'The Jews or the Romans probably had the body all the time.' (For example: they had only to produce it, to make the disciples look silly; they clearly had no idea what was going on; thousands of people believed the apostles, and they made no attempt to disprove the story.)

When they give you three satisfactory reasons, give them the fourth digit.

This may sound complicated! But it's great fun, and introduces a competitive element which makes people think very carefully indeed about the arguments and their validity. Make sure you take five or 10 minutes at the end of the exercise to debrief and re-emphasise the most important points.

THE RESURRECTION

'He (Jesus) was delivered over to death for our sins and was raised to life for our justification.'
Romans 4:25

'...Because we know that the one who raised the Lord Jesus from the dead will also raise us with Jesus and present us with you in his presence.'
2 Corinthians 4:14

'And if the Spirit of him who raised Jesus from the dead is living in you, he who raised Christ from the dead will also give life to your mortal bodies through his Spirit, who lives in you.'
Romans 8:11

'...That power is like the working of his mighty strength, which he exerted in Christ when he raised him from the dead and seated him at his right hand in the heavenly realms...'
Ephesians 1:19b-20

'Who will bring any charge against those whom God has chosen? It is God who justifies. Who is he that condemns? Christ Jesus, who died - more than that, who was raised to life - is at the right hand of God and is also interceding for us.'
Romans 8:33-34

'Since, then, you have been raised with Christ, set your hearts on things above, where Christ is seated at the right hand of God.'
Colossians 3:1.

(all verses from the NIV Bible)

Why do these scripture passages say the resurrection is so vital?

....

What difference does the resurrection make to us now?

....

SO WHAT?
(15 mins)
Either staying in mini-groups, or coming back together, have a look at six important New Testament statements about the resurrection. Hand out copies of the worksheet, but also ensure that the group have access to Bibles, so that they can look up the passages from which these statements are drawn, and examine the context.

Allow 10 minutes on the sheet then ask for feedback – which should include: 'The resurrection is important because it proves we're right with God (Romans 4:24); guarantees that we'll live again after death (2 Corinthians 4:14); brings us the new life we have in Jesus (Romans 8:11); shows us where Jesus is today (Ephesians 1:20); means that God will never condemn us (Romans 8:34); and gives us a reason for living a new lifestyle (Colossians 3:1).'

WRAP-UP
(5 mins)
If it's appropriate, end with a brief time of prayer together. Ask people to close their eyes and just let the realisation flood through them that if all this is true, they are actually now in the presence of somebody *living* and really here! Then talk simply and briefly to him, thanking him for his triumphant resurrection and his constant presence with us today.

GUIDANCE

MEETING AIM:

To help the group realise that God wants to influence and guide them in their daily decision-making and to teach them that the Bible contains God's directions for living.

STREET ORIENTEERING
(60-80 mins)

This activity is best done as a linked social/fun event, before the meeting proper or even the week before as a prelude to the teaching.

In teams of three or four, groups are sent out on foot to work out clues and complete a course in the neighbouring streets/area. Questions are based on your locality, eg: How many steps at the entrance to the White Hart Hotel? What colour is the front door at 18 Ash Road?

This will require you to do considerable preparation. The question sheet should incorporate a simple map and could include cryptic clues (but don't make it too hard).

Wrong or missing answers incur a time penalty; the winning team is the one which completes the course fastest. The results and prizes can be given out the following week...this gives you time to check out the answers from the different teams and tot up any time penalties. It also provides an incentive for the youth group to attend that following week.

N.B. Be aware of the potential safety hazards of this activity and take steps to reduce the risks. Insist that the group always stays together when out, so that individuals do not get isolated, lost or worse! Also underline the importance of road safety - in their haste you don't want them getting run over. Include your phone number on the question/map sheet and ensure each group has enough money or a phone card to phone you if they hit a problem or emergency. Make sure this exercise is done in daylight hours and that the group come suitably clothed. Finally, you must inform the parents and get their permission.

I know this all seems a bit of a drag - but it is important to avoid fun turning into tragedy.

GAME OPTIONS
(15 mins)

(Choose one or two from this selection of games which link into the theme of guidance)

WHAT'S NEXT?

This is a song lyric quiz which will be popular with your group if they are into chart music. The game works best with small groups of three or four in a team - each group will need paper and a pen. Write onto large cards or OHP sheets two or three lines from current chart singles. The teams have to write down the next line of the song.

Use 'Top 10' chart music plus a few popular songs from the last few years. For current chart lyrics buy *Smash Hits* magazine - but beware of using songs with overtly sexual or offensive language.

PEGGED OUT

This is lots of fun and uses simple props. You need blindfolds, two chairs, a bucket and 30 or more clothes pegs. Sitting opposite each other with knees just touching, two people are blindfolded. A bucket of pegs is placed by their feet and they have 40 seconds to reach down and fix as many pegs onto each other (not themselves) as they can. When the time is up the pair stand, and the pegs still hanging onto their clothes, hair or skin are counted. After other two-somes have tried, the pair with the highest number are declared the winners.

BLIND BARROWS

In teams of two, one opts to be a barrow (walking on their hands), while their partner lifts their legs and steers them. The 'barrow' is blindfolded and relies for direction on the shouted advice of their partner. Teams compete in lanes down the room/hall in a straight race. To add an extra element of fun put equal numbers of paper plates in each lane containing large chunks of Turkish delight, marshmallows or chocolate. The barrow must stop and eat each plateful before completing the course. A further variation is to do away with lanes and fill the course with obstacles - cushions, empty cardboard boxes, etc - which the teams must negotiate.

BACK TO THE FUTURE
(5 mins)

While everyone gets their breath back after the games, show a short clip from one of the three *Back To The Future* videos, or choose another film which contains an element of time travel. Use this as an introduction to talking about the advantages of being able to travel ahead or back in time to alter a bad decision.

I DID IT GOD'S WAY
(10 mins)

In small groups get them to check out the following scriptures and identify as many instructions from God on how to live and make decisions as they can. Get them to jot them down on a pad.

1 Chronicles 28:8-10; Proverbs 3:5-6; Matthew 6:33-34; 1 Peter 5:5-9.

When the groups feedback underline any conditions behind the promises in these verses.

LOOKING FORWARD, LOOKING BACK
(15-20 mins)

Hand out copies of the activity sheet opposite and a pen to each individual. Ask them to draw four mini-pictures which represent four significant things or events in their lives so far. Then ask them to share in small groups what they have drawn and why it was important and memorable. Make sure an adult worker is in each of the small groups.

Then get them to draw three more mini-pictures representing dreams or ambitions they have for the future. After a few minutes ask them to share what they have drawn and why it means a lot to them.

GOD'S WILL
(10 mins)

Referring to the pictures that they have drawn tell them that God has a record of our lives so far and that he knows us better than we know ourselves. Read out Psalm 139:1-16,23-24, which is a moving account of God's interest and appreciation of each individual.

SAY:

'You might think you are insignificant, but God knows us, loves us, and has plans for each one of our lives. He wants us to live fulfilled lives' (John 10:10).

Refer back to Provers 3:5-6 explaining that if we trust in God and ask him to guide us he promises us to direct our future.

Close this meeting by inviting everyone to kneel and hold the pictures they drew earlier in their outstretched arms. Explain what you are about to do, and then pray, asking God to take each individual's ambitions and plans for the future (name them, be specific). Ask him to show the person if that is what he wants for them and their future, and if not to reveal the way ahead.

Draw 4 pictures which represent 4 significant things in your life so far (they don't have to be works of art!)

Draw 3 pictures which represent dreams or ambitions you have for the future.

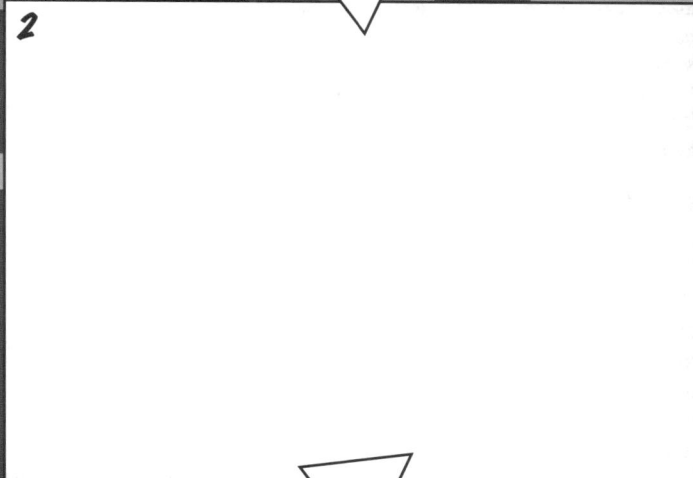

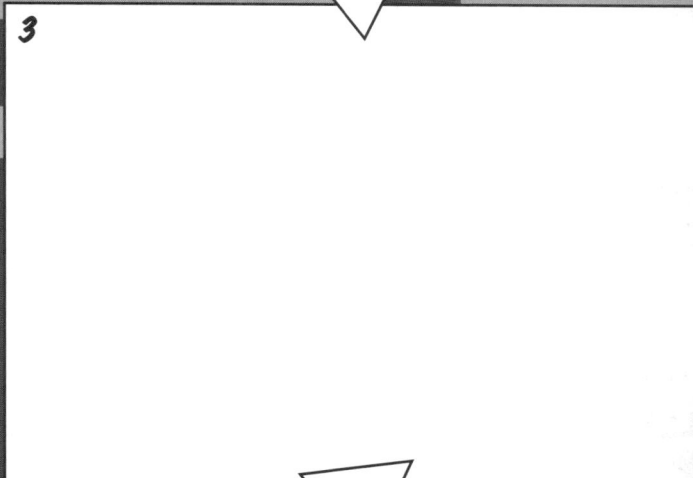

1

1

2

2

3

3

4

SUFFERING

MEETING AIM:

To help your group see that Christians have some answers to the problem of suffering.

The outline looks at four key answers to the question, 'Why does suffering exist?' Most of the activities are potentially fairly riotous, because otherwise the subject matter could make it a gloomy, heavy session. But be sensitive to the possibility that the discussion may become more serious, intimate and personal than you anticipate (especially if someone present has a history of family tragedy). If so, be ready to abandon the 'fun' features and simply deal with the issues being raised.

INSTANT SOAP (10-15 mins)

Begin by splitting the group into teams of four, five or six. Explain that *Brookside* is slipping in the ratings, *Home and Away* is being discontinued, and *Neighbours* has lost its touch. They have to design the plot for a new gritty, sensational soap opera, right through its first six episodes. They can call it what they like, but they must include as much disaster and human suffering as possible. The more catastrophes, the higher the ratings will go. If time allows, you could also ask them to act out the opening episode.

As the groups report back, list on a flip-chart the number of different catastrophes they come up with. After rewarding the winners, make the point that life is full of many kinds of suffering - and it fascinates us. That's why gory operations on *Casualty* pull millions of viewers.

But is there any reason for it all? Or is human suffering just a mystery? The Bible suggests at least four answers.

LEMMINGS LIVE (10-15 mins)

Most people have played the computer game 'Lemmings'. (Even if they haven't, they'll soon pick it up.) Use the whole group to play Lemmings live. Most will be Lemmings - three or four can be controllers. Design your own course with plenty of pitfalls and opportunities for Lemmings to die (not literally!) before reaching 'home'.

Give the controllers big stickers saying 'Blocker', 'Builder', 'Nuke', etc, and a horn to sound which means 'I am zapping this level'. When the Lemmings emerge from their trapdoor, walking in an agreed direction, the controllers dash about and slap on badges to try to get the Lemmings heading homeward without accident.

They can shout 'Pause' to freeze everything while they discuss tactics, but they can do this only twice.

If none of this makes any sense to you, design the game in consultation with someone in the group who has played Lemmings. There should be plenty of them!

After you have played enough, say: God could have designed us to be Lemmings - completely obedient to the control of a master-planner with a finger on the button - but he didn't.

Lemmings are silly, mindless creatures. God gave us more dignity; he gave us personal freedom (Read Psalm 8:4-6).

So we make *wrong* choices too - which may lead to suffering. The responsibility is ours. Lemmings can't be blamed for jumping over a cliff. Human beings *can* be blamed for smoking cigarettes and suffering lung cancer.

REWRITING THE STORY (10-15 mins)

Because humans have chosen wrongly, there's something wrong with their basic nature which the Bible calls *sin*. Sin is an internal bias that keeps us going wrong (read Romans 7:21-23). Distribute copies of the worksheet opposite to small groups and allow them up to six minutes to re-write the stories. Then get some feed back from each group.

Then sum up this section by explaining that this is the Bible's second explanation for suffering: much of it is caused by our sinful nature. Even seeming natural disasters (eg the Ethiopian famine) often come from human sin (the irresponsible greed which led to misuse of land and desertification).

SWITCH (10 mins)

Now play a game with two teams and a ball. Each team has a goal at their end of the room, consisting of a cardboard box into which the ball can be dropped. There are three sets of rules:

(a) ANYTHING GOES. Each team tries to get the ball into the opponents' goal by any means possible.

(b) QUITE THE REVERSE. Each team tries to get the ball into their own goal, but must drop the ball whenever touched by an opponent.

(c) LINK UP. Team members stand back to back, linking arms in pairs, and each pair then tries to get the ball into the opponents' goal without unlinking their arms.

Keep blowing a whistle and suddenly switching the rules. It will take a while

before people get used to it, and the possibilities of confusion are enormous. (Add to them by giving lots of penalties, sending-offs, etc.)

At the end point out that this can be a very frustrating and funny game because you can't rely on the rules - the laws keep changing. Some people wonder why God doesn't stop aeroplanes crashing or volcanoes erupting. Part of the answer is that we live in a universe of unchanging, regular natural law - and it's a good thing we do. Would you feel safer or less safe if God kept changing the rules?

Suppose you left home one morning and found gravity had been reversed? If every time someone jumped over a cliff, the rocks turned to jelly; or every time someone tried to light a cigarette, it floated away in the sky. God wouldn't be respecting our freedom. He doesn't make life artificially soft.

THE DEEPEST DIMENSION (10 mins)

But even this doesn't explain all suffering. Read Romans 8:18-23, and in small groups discuss:

● Is this world running the way God wants it to, or is something wrong? If so what?

● What will be the answer to the problems of this planet?

● The world is in a mess, but Christians have a happy time. Which verse here says that this claim is total nonsense?

CONCLUSION (5-10 mins)

Explain that this is the fourth answer: that human sin spoiled God's plan for creation (Genesis 3:16-19) and so the world isn't working in the way it should. Suffering has crept into life because God's planet has been hijacked. We can't prove this - but it makes more sense than believing that all life is the way it should be (as New Agers tend to claim); or that all life is purposeless, painful and a cynical joke (if we really believed that, we'd all be committing suicide).

For Christians who know the reality of God in their lives, there are no glib answers - suffering is still a mystery - but there can be a firm conviction that God knows best, and that some day 'the glory that is to be revealed' will make sense of it all.

End with a time of prayer for people who are suffering. Get the group to suggest some ideas.

ALTERNATIVE VERSION

Hurley left bewildered by Grant's escapade

By Rebecca Pike

ELIZABETH HURLEY said last night that she was "bewildered and saddened" after the arrest of her boyfriend, Hugh Grant, on charges of lewd conduct with a Los Angeles prostitute.

Miss Hurley issued a statement as she was on her way to the West Country. She has a home at West Littleton, near Bath. Grant, 34, is expected to fly in from America.

"I am still bewildered and saddened by recent events and have not been in a fit state to make any decisions about my future," she said.

"For years I have turned to Hugh for help during difficult times and so now, even though my family and friends have been kind, I am very much alone.

"This is all very painful for me and if members of the press could find it in their hearts to give me some time to think, I would be grateful."

Miss Hurley, 29, made her appeal for privacy after being constantly pursued by reporters since the news of Grant's arrest.

The actress and model is launching herself as the new face of Esteé Lauder for a £1 million fee. She spent the day meeting department store buyers and beauty editors to launch the company's new range of perfume, Pleasures.

Miss Hurley had been asked whether she would prefer to postpone the launch to avoid a media stampede — but she decided to press ahead with it.

Afterwards, a beauty editor said of the publicity surrounding Grant's arrest: "This has come at a very opportune moment for both of them.

"It will keep her in the public eye for longer. It is exactly what she is all about. This one will run and run."

Read these two newspaper stories, then as a group rewrite the stories imagining the people concerned were perfect. How different would they sound?

Sisters clubbed to death before house burned

TWO elderly sisters were battered to death before their house was set on fire, police disclosed last night.

The intruder used a blunt instrument to attack Elsie Gregory, 72, and Aileen Dudhill, 79.

Firefighters and police were called to the house in Rotherham, South Yorks, when a neighbour saw smoke coming from a rear window.

Officers broke in and found the women's bodies in the sitting room.

"I am horrified at what I have seen," said Det Supt Bob Purdy. "It is a terrible, despicable crime.

"Property in the house has been disturbed so it is a reasonable assumption that robbery might have been the motive.

"There is no evidence of forced entry but I believe that someone else has been in the house."

The two women lived with Mrs Dudhill's husband from the 1940s and ran a grocery store together.

The sisters continued to manage the store after Mr Dudhill died about 30 years ago. They moved to their current home about 12 years ago and became members of Neighbourhood Watch.

Less than four hours before the killing, Mrs Dudhill took her regular Sunday stroll to a roadside bench to enjoy the afternoon sunshine.

She walked with the aid of a stick. Her sister, who was just 5ft tall, had a stoop caused by severe curvature of the spine.

Neighbours said youths had been seen in the road earlier that day drinking beer.

Sean Page, an insurance broker, said: "What has happened is sickening. They were the sweetest old ladies you could hope to meet.

"I moved here with my family two years ago and they sent us a card out of the blue wishing us well and saying that they hoped we enjoyed living in our new home.

"To think anyone would do something like this is appalling. It is a respectable area.

"We don't have much trouble and this has come as an absolute shock."

Victor De Roeck, 82, said: "We often saw the ladies gardening. They were delightful. They even sent birthday cards to my three dogs.

"They were just such lovely people and it's a shock to think that someone could do this."

APOLOGETICS

MEETING AIM:
To help the group practise some arguments in defence of important Christian beliefs so that when they get interested or aggressive questions about their faith, they will have some coherent answers to give.

PREPARATION
This outline involves more preparation than usual. You can't teach teenagers to defend their faith without a degree of effort and study on your part.

SILLY REASONS (10-15 mins)
Photocopy the sheet opposite and then cut up the boxes so that you end up one 'Q' card and one 'A' card for every three members of your group.

Then divide people into groups of three and issue each small group with one 'Q' and one 'A' card at random. They then have three minutes to think of a convincing way of showing why their 'answer' card contains the logical response to their 'question' card. They then present their story to everyone.

A panel of judges votes on whether they have given a good answer or not. This is pretty silly, and too many long stories can eat away your time. Keep it short.

Then say: 'That was all about silly answers to questions. And about thinking on your feet when you don't have a clue what answer to give. All too often, Christians give silly answers to people who attack their faith, because they haven't worked out how to defend it...'

COMPLETE THE SENTENCE (10 mins)
Give people slips of paper each containing the half-sentences below and ask them to complete them.

'I think the way I defend my faith is really...'
'The question I have most trouble with is...'
'I sometimes don't say what I should because...'

Some groups might wish to share and discuss the answers. Other groups might prefer this to be a personal, private exercise.

HOW TO DEFEND (10 mins)
Put on the OHP an acetate containing this jumble of adverbs:

**GENTLY LOUDLY RESPECTFULLY
WISELY DECIDEDLY BRIGHTLY
HAPPILY SOLEMNLY LOGICALLY**

**PROMPTLY SHREWDLY
DEFENSIVELY AGGRESSIVELY**

Give each sub-group three Bible references: 1 Peter 3:15-16; Colossians 4:5-6; Acts 17:2. Ask them to decide: (a) Which of these words describe how we should defend our faith - according to the verses? (b) Are there other words which we'd add, after reading each passage? Share your results before moving on.

WHEN TO DEFEND (15 mins)
Now ask each sub-group to think of a situation in which it wouldn't be a good idea to defend their faith, and to make up an instant drama sketch about somebody who tries anyway.

Some ideas you might suggest as examples: when the other person is really in a hurry; when you've just done something cataclysmically idiotic and your reputation is zero; when the other person isn't really interested in the topic anyway.

After a few minutes, perform the sketches to one another (it doesn't matter if they're extremely rough).

Then discuss: (a) What should have happened in this situation? (b) When is the right time and how do we know?

WHAT TO SAY (15-20 mins)
Explain that there are two common kinds of attacks:

MISSILE 1 - 'That's just your opinion; other people may think differently.'
MISSILE 2 - 'That may be Christianity, but it's stupid.'

To defend yourself against Missile 1 you must be able to prove that your beliefs really are in the Bible.

If the group is reasonably biblically literate, give them a list of key Christian claims (eg that God is personal, that Jesus is the Son of God, that he rose from the dead), and ask them to brainstorm passages which they could use to prove that these claims truly are biblical.

If the group is less confident, give them a list of verses to find which will illustrate one or other of these claims, and ask them to link up each verse with the claim it illustrates.

To cope with Missile 2 you need to know what are the common arguments people launch against Christianity.

Ask the group to shoot out all the arguments and objections they can think of -

and write them down on the OHP as they are suggested. Then vote on the top seven.

Promise that you will mail to them tomorrow a postcard containing the list of seven top objections, and ask them to look at the list throughout the week - working out answers to as many as they can. Suggest sources from which they could find answers. Have some books available to borrow (see list below).

This approach is much better than spoonfeeding them with answers or trying to construct responses in discussion on the spot. When people wrestle with these problems over a few days, the solutions they discover will be more reflective, better considered - and remembered longer. Resist the temptation to make it too easy for them!

AND FINALLY... (10 mins)
Write two proverbs on the OHP:

1. **'Honesty is the best defence.'**
2. **'The best form of defence is attack.'**

There are still two questions to answer. First: What about the questions you honestly can't answer? Explain that 'honesty is the best defence'. We should say three things: 'I don't know' (integrity); 'But I'll find out' (open-mindedness); 'And then I'll tell you' (commitment).

Second, how do we turn defence into attack? It's important that we don't just answer question after question until the non-Christian tires of it. We must launch a counter-attack. For instance after answering the question, 'What will happen to all those who haven't heard the gospel?' you could change gear by saying, 'But how about those who have heard? You've understood clearly and you haven't responded. If it's true, where does that leave you...?'

Give the sub-groups one objection each from the 'top seven'. Give them five minutes to think of a way of switching from defence to attack after answering the question.

End by summarising the session's key points (there were quite a few). And pray for all the battles the group may face in the coming week.

For some answers, check out: *It Makes Sense* By Steve Gaukroger (SU), *You Must Be Joking* by Michael Green (Hodder), *Explaining Your Faith* by Alister McGrath (IVP), *Evidence That Demands A Verdict* by Josh McDowell.

Q Why did Japan lose World War 2?	Q Why are Take That so talented?	Q Why are ladybirds called ladybirds?	Q Why do we drive on the left-hand side of the road in the UK?
Q Why are dogs' noses cold?	Q Why are public schools private?	Q Why is Cardiff the capital of Wales?	Q Why does the mother of the bride wear a hat?
A Because Cilla Black has never appeared on Channel 4.	A Because it is hotter in India than Greenland.	A Because my mum said so.	A Because Mrs Thatcher is no longer the prime minister.
A Because apples are less fattening than chocolate.	A Because you can't help licking your lips when eating a doughnut.	A Because of Einstein's theory of time and space.	A Because more people buy red cars than brown.
A Because Brazilians are so good at playing football.	A Because the lady loves to eat Milk Tray.		

EVANGELISM

MEETING AIM:
To show that Christ commands us all to spread the gospel; and to encourage the group to identify creative and culturally sensitive ways to evangelise their friends.

PREPARATION
Try to read the book *It Makes Sense* By Stephen Gaukroger (Scripture Union) before you lead this meeting. It will help you prepare for possible 'But what about...' questions which may arise when you talk about common objections to the gospel. It is also a good book to loan or give to members of your group.

WHAT'S MY JOB?
(5 mins)
Before the meeting pre-arrange with a member of your group for them to play the role of a well-known evangelist (eg Billy Graham, Luis Palau) in this adapted form of the golden oldie TV panel game 'What's My Line?' Brief the young person thoroughly so they understand the role and ministry of a full-time evangelist.

Then at the meeting the 'evangelist' is hidden away while the young people have 20 questions to discover the job and if possible, identify the person. Their questions must be phrased so the hidden person only has to reply 'yes' or 'no'.

WHAT'S THE DIFFERENCE?
(5 mins)
ASK:
What is the difference between an evangelist, evangelism, and an evangelical Christian? These three terms are commonly jumbled together. If you are unsure of the answer yourself order a copy of *Who do Evangelicals think they are?* by Clive Calver, Ian Coffey and Peter Meadows (95p) published by the Evangelical Alliance (Tel: 0171-582 0228).

GREAT COMMISSION
(5 mins)
Get a member of the group to read out Matthew 28:16-20.
SAY: When someone is dying or about to leave their friends for a long time, their last words are very important. These verses record Jesus' last words before he left his disciples for heaven. These words were his last instructions to them.

Jesus told his followers that he would continue to be with them - but how?

And how long do these instructions to evangelise and baptise apply for?

BEST AND WORST
(15 mins)
Hand out copies of the cartoon worksheet and pens and give your young people three minutes to make their decisions on the best and worst ways to evangelise their friends. Then ask them to draw or write down any other styles of witnessing and evangelism which they think would be appropriate.

As they feedback their opinions and ideas, encourage group discussion, have someone take notes, and keep both eyes wide open for creative evangelism ideas. Be sure to encourage every suggestion - even those that seem wacky or unrealistic.

Use this exercise to discuss the ways church members reach out to their non-Christian friends and unchurched young people in the district. Try to avoid it becoming a 'moan' about what the church doesn't do, but instead a positive and open discussion of what the church *could* do.

If your church has one or more persons specifically responsible for the evangelism programme, it would be good to invite them to this meeting, mainly to listen to the young people. If they can't come, be sure to brief them about what the young people say or, even better, get one of the group to meet the person or committee, with you present for moral support.

LIFESAVER
(15-20 mins)
During the week before this meeting keep an eye on the newspapers and cut out any stories about someone risking or losing their own life to save someone else.

Hand out photocopies of the stories, or photocopy onto acetate and project them on a whiteboard or wall. Read out the stories and use them as a springboard to discuss the following questions.

Would you risk your own life to save -
● a baby? ● your pet dog/cat?
● someone you love? ● an old person?
● a convicted criminal?

Allow some discussion/debate and then talk for three minutes about the death of Jesus - how he voluntarily died in great pain so that the human race could be saved from eternal death and separation from God. Depending on your group, it may be appropriate to invite people to respond to Christ and become Christians. Make sure you have some clear, well written leaflets explaining what becoming a Christian involves, which you can hand out to anyone interested.

WITNESSING OBJECTIONS
(10 mins)
Listed below are the most common reasons for young Christians holding back from witnessing to their friends. Look through the list and prepare your response prior to the meeting.

Write out the list below and ask them as individuals, or in small groups, to prepare an answer to one of the views. As well as reasoned argument encourage them to quote some Bible verses to back up their views if possible.

● 'I feel like I am imposing my views on other people.'
● 'I will look like a fool.'
● 'They won't listen to me.'
● 'I don't know enough about the Christian faith.'
● 'It's the job of an evangelist, not me, to tell people the gospel.'

Useful source verses include: 2 Peter 3:15; 2 Timothy 4:1-2; 1 Thessalonians 2:6-8.

ACTION PRAYERS
(5 mins)
Encourage the group to think about one friend whom they could talk to about their faith in the next seven days. Then get them praying for an opportunity to witness to their friend, and for the right words to say. Depending on your group, you'll know whether this will work best on their own quietly; in small groups, take it in turn to pray; or by writing down the first name of the person on a slip of paper, then collecting the names and one person praying, mentioning the names in turn.

Allow some feedback time next week for people to share whether their prayer for a chance to witness got answered.

The Christian Service Centre publishes an annually updated manual which lists Christian organisations which provide mission/service opportunities in the UK and abroad. The Short-Term Service (STS) Directory is available for £4.74 from CSC, Holloway Street West, Lower Gornal, Dudley, West Midlands DY3 2DZ (Tel: 01902 882836).

THE SECOND COMING

MEETING AIM:

To demystify what the Bible says about Jesus' coming-again, and the events surrounding it. To give people a little understanding of the arguments which rage about it. And to provoke them to think where they would stand should Jesus come back today.

GUESS THE ENDING
(10 mins)

Divide people into groups, and distribute to each group a piece of paper containing these half-sentences:

'The ancient Aztec Indian cure for a boil on the bottom is...'

'If any one will not wash his feet, let him be...'

'So the Archbishop said to the Queen, "If you want my advice, what you really ought to do about Charles and Diana is..."'

Give four minutes to find appropriate endings to each sentence. Award a small prize for the funniest, most apt, or most realistic. Then say: 'Humans are always looking for appropriate endings. We don't like TV series that finish with the plot unresolved. We can't resist sneaking a look at the last page of the book to see how it all comes out. We like endings to wrap everything up in an appropriate way.'

Read out this list of dates, and ask what all these years have in common?

195; 365; 1000; 1030; 1033; 1492; 1496; 1524; 1588; 1666; 1822; 1834; 1843 1874; 1882 1911; 1920; 1924; 1925; 1936; 1953; 1969; 1972; 1982; 1991.

The answer is:
They're all years in which the end of the world was supposed to happen, according to one prophet or another! People never stop guessing about endings. But the Bible does give us certain information about Jesus' coming back, and what will happen thereafter. In this session we'll explore some of it.

PREDICTIONS
(10 mins)

Hand out copies of the worksheet opposite and allow your group five to eight minutes to answer the question. Then read out the answers and use the results to re-emphasise the key features of the 'Last Things',

according to Scripture: the sudden return of Jesus, and our rising to meet him; the judgement of Christians and non-Christians; the future of the planet.

SIGNS OF THE END
(10 mins)

Jesus will return at a time when we're not expecting him. But when? His disciples asked for some clues, and Jesus gave them Matthew 24:3-14. (Read it together - and maybe verses 23-31 too.)

Give each small group a pile of recent newspapers, a large sheet of paper, and some Prittstick. Ask them to look again at the signs Jesus mentioned, and to cut out from the papers any headlines which refer to these kinds of thing taking place in our day.

After a few minutes, stop and see what you've got. The chances are that there will be lots! Headlines about war, famine, earthquakes and cults aren't unusual - and they never have been. Says Stephen Travis: 'These are signs which we can expect right through the period from the resurrection of Jesus till his final coming...Jesus' aim in telling us these signs was not to satisfy our curiosity, but to strengthen faith and warn of dangers that Christian can expect' (*The Jesus Hope* Word Books). We shouldn't use these headlines to try to calculate exact dates, but to give us the reassurance that, despite all the evil and wrong in the world, Jesus truly is coming back, and all these disasters just bear witness to it.

A MATTER OF JUDGEMENT
(10 mins)

One of the solemn realities of the Second Coming is that it ushers in God's judgement. Read two passages that speak about the judgement of believers - 2 Corinthians 5:8-10 and 1 Corinthians 3:11-15 - and one that speaks about the judgement of unbelievers - Revelation 20:12-15

ASK: what's different about the two situations?

Then look at three case studies...

Case Study One:

Alistair was never a Christian. Although he was brought up in a Christian family who attended an evangelical church, he always resisted making a commitment to Jesus because he had plans of his own. When he was killed suddenly in a road accident at the age of 23, he couldn't have told you what he

believed. The one thing that was sure was this: he was simply living to have a good time and enjoy himself.

Case Study Two:

Gina dropped out of the church when she went to university. It wasn't that she didn't believe, just that her once-fervent faith had gone stone cold. After a couple of terms she moved out of the halls of residence to live with her boyfriend, and from that day forth she never opened her Bible again. Occasionally, though, she felt twinges of guilt and a wistful longing to be right with God again. It seemed the Holy Spirit hadn't given up on her. But he still hadn't got through when one day she had a sudden heart attack and died.

Case Study Three:

Colin had lived a pretty dreadful, self-centred life, and had ruined the lives of all those who cared for him. His mother died broken-hearted, and his two wives had finally walked out, having had enough. His kids didn't speak to him any more, especially when his wild lifestyle led to his contracting full-blown AIDS. That experience made him think seriously for the first time in his life. He started talking to the vicar who visited the hospice where he was slowly dying. The night before his life ebbed away, he asked God to forgive his sin. There wasn't time, though, to do anything about the trail of destruction and evil he had left behind him.

Ask the groups to decide, 'How will these people stand in the judgement? What will God have to say to them? Is that what you would say, if you were God?

BACK TO THE FUTURE
(10 mins)

Two things are certain. First, *someone* in your church will have a copy of Larry Norman's great song 'I Wish We'd All Been Ready' (it was a massive Christian hit). Secondly, few of your kids will ever have heard it before! To end the session and get them to think about their own response to the teaching they've explored today, simply get someone to read out Matthew 24:37-42, then play the song. (Put the words up on OHP to give them something to look at.) Leave a few moments for quiet, individual response - then pray together.

PRE·DICTIONS

A massive bomb will destroy all known life except for the Christians

JESUS will come back + Christians will rise to the air to meet HIM.

The earth will B burned UP

WHICH OF? THESE DOES THE BIBLE SAY WILL HAPPEN

All evil powers will B destroyed

The living + the dead will B judged

The devil will reign for a thousand years

A plague of frogs invade Asia and Africa

There will B a new heaven and a new earth

IF U·R UNSURE, CHECK OUT THESE VERSES WHICH WILL HELP U ON SOME OF THE ABOVE
2 Peter 3:10-13 * Revelation 20:12-15 * 1 Thess 4:16-18

YOUTH WORK

'It encourages you to think strategically and long-term and yet offers "life-savers" when in the short-term you are panicking! I read it, I use it, I recommend it.'

HEATHER BOYD
Harrow Churches Schools
Link Worker

'It's got the lot!'

STEVE MALLON
Church of Scotland
Youth Adviser

- -

DON'T MISS OUT ON A SINGLE COPY - SUBSCRIBE TODAY

For just £22.80* we'll deliver YOUTH**WORK** to your door every month. Complete the simple direct debit form below and we'll send you FREE OF CHARGE *Nurturing Young Disciples* by John Buckeridge (worth £6.99).

Complete this form and send to:
YOUTH**WORK**, Freepost, 37 Elm Road, New Malden, Surrey KT3 3BR.

NAME...

ADDRESS...

....

....

POSTCODE ....

■■■■ OPTION ONE ■■■■

I would like to subscribe by Direct Debit - and get my FREE copy of *Nurturing Young Disciples* by John Buckeridge - £22.80* for 1 year (12 issues)

To the manager of

_____bank.

Address (of bank)

_____

_____

Postcode _____

Sort Code ☐☐ / ☐☐ / ☐☐

Account No.

☐☐☐☐☐☐☐☐

Name of account holder(s):

_____

_____

I/We authorise you until further notice in writing to charge my / our account with unspecified amounts which Trinity Square Ltd may debit thereto by Direct debit in respect of my / our annual magazine subscription.

Signed _____

Office Use - Originators No.
954471 Reference No._____

■■■■ OPTION TWO ■■■■

I would like to subscribe to YOUTH**WORK** for 1 year *(12 issues)* and pay by cheque or credit card

i) I enclose my cheque / Postal Order for £22.80* *(payable to Trinity Square Ltd)*

ii) Please debit my Visa / Mastercard for £22.80*:

Card No. ☐☐☐☐

☐☐☐☐☐☐☐☐

☐☐☐☐

Expiry date ☐☐ / ☐☐

Signed_____

If you have any enquiries or difficulties please phone 0181-942 9761 and ask for Subscriptions.

* These prices apply up to 1 April 1997. After this date prices may vary - phone 0181-942 9761 to check.

All prices are one year UK only. For overseas subscriptions please pay by credit card or sterling draft only. Europe £34.30*. Rest of the World £35.90*. Trinity Square Ltd is registered under the Data Protection Act 1984 and holds names and addresses for the purposes of mailing details of goods and services. Details on request.

☐ Tick here if you do not wish to receive mailings from other companies.

HBYY